Dear Book Lover,

Jan Karon is one of the most beloved authors writing today. In her popular *Mitford* books, she has created a charming community that readers love to visit again and again. One of her most memorable characters is that of Father Tim Kavanagh. His good nature, gentle wit, and wisdom have guided townsfolk through mishaps and heartaches, joys and celebrations. For years, Father Tim has relied on his leather bound, dog-eared journals, which he has lovingly filled with words of faith and encouragement gleaned from his favorite thinkers.

Now you can have a copy of the book that Father Tim keeps close by his side in our exclusive Doubleday Large Print edition! We've kept the endearing notes in Father Tim's own "handwriting" and then transcribed his entries on the facing page in easy-to-read large print. We sincerely hope you enjoy this special club edition, a book to be enjoyed, treasured, and shared with loved ones for years to come.

Jennifer Hufford

Happy reading!
Jennifer Hufford
Editor, Doubleday Large Print

I have gathered a posy of other men's flowers, and nothing but the thread that binds them is mine own.

John Bartlett

I have gathered a posy of
other men's flowers, and
nothing but the thread that
binds them is mine own.

John Bartlett

. . . the cheerful heart has a continual feast.

Proverbs 15:15 NIV

. . . the cheerful heart has a continual feast.

Proverbs 15:15 NIV

The first rule is to keep an untroubled spirit. The second is to look things in the face and know them for what they are.

Marcus Aurelius

The first rule is to keep an
untroubled spirit. The second is
to look things in the face and
know them for what they are.

Marcus Aurelius

Do not look forward to what may happen tomorrow; the same everlasting Father who cares for you today will take care of you tomorrow and every day. *Either He will shield you from suffering, or He will give you unfailing strength to bear it.* Be at peace, then, put aside all anxious thoughts and imaginations, and say continually: "The Lord is my strength and my shield; my heart has trusted in Him and I am helped. He is not only with me . . . but in me . . . and I in Him."

—St. Francis de Sales

Do not look forward to what may
happen tomorrow; the same everlasting Father who cares for you
today wiill take care of you
tomorrow and every day. <u>Either</u>
<u>He will shield you from suffer-</u>
<u>ing, or He will giive you unfail-</u>
<u>iing strength to bear it.</u> Be at
peace, then, put aside all anxious
thoughts and imagiinations, and
say continually: "The Lord is my
strength and my shield; my heart
has trusted in Him and I am helped. He is not only with me . . .
but iin me . . . and I in Him."

     --St. Francis de Sales

There is but one way to tranquility of mind and happiness. Let this therefore be always ready at hand with thee, both when thou wakest early in the morning, and when thou goest late to sleep, to account no external thing thine own, but commit all these to God.

—Epictetus

There is but one way to tranquiil-
ity af mind and happiness. Let
this therefore be always ready at
hand wiith thee, both when thou
wakest early iin the morning,
and when thou goest late to
sleep, to account no external
thiing thine own, but commit
all these to God.

--Epictetus

Happy the man, and happy he alone, who can call today his own; He who is secure within can say, tomorrow do thy worst, for I have lived today.

John Dryden

Nothing is worth more than this day.

Goethe

Happy the man, and happy he alone, who can call today his own; He who is secure within can say, tomorrow do thy worst, for I have lived today.

John Dryden

Nothing is worth more than this day.

Goethe

Sometimes you've got to jump off cliffs and grow wings on the way down.

—Ray Bradbury

proposal to C!!

Duty is ours; events are God's.

—Samuel Rutherford

Start by doing what's necessary, then what's possible, and suddenly you are doing the impossible.

—Francis of Assisi

Sometimes you've got to jump
off cliffs and grow wings on
the way down.

— Ray Bradbury

proposal to C !!

Duty is ours; events are God's.

— Samuel Rutherford

Start by doing what's necessary,
then what's possible, and
suddenly you are doing the
impossible.

— Francis of Assisi

Though other friends walk by your side,
Yet sometimes it must surely be,
They wonder where your thoughts have
    gone
Because I have you here with me.

And when the busy day is done
And work is ended, voices cease
When everyone has said goodnight,
In fading firelight, then in peace

I idly rest: you come to me,
Your dear love holds me close to you.
If I could see you face to face
It would not be more sweet and true.

—Sarah Orne Jewett (1849–1909)

C in NYC

Though other friends walk by your
side,
Yet sometimes it must surely be,
They wonder where your thoughts
have gone
Because I have you here with me.

And when the busy day is done
And work is ended, voices cease
When everyone has said goodnight,
In fading firelight, then in peace

I idly rest: you come to me,
Your dear love holds me close
to you.
If I could see you face to face
It would not be more sweet
and true.

— Sarah Orne Jewett (1849–1909)

C in NYC

The danger for most of us lies not in setting our aim too high and falling short, but in setting our aim too low, and achieving our mark.

Michelangelo Buonarroti, 1475–1564

We don't stop playing because we grow old; we grow old because we stop playing.

Geo Bernard Shaw

The danger for most of us lies
not in setting our aim too high
and falling short, but in setting
our aim too low, and achieving
our mark.

Michelangelo Buonarroti, 1475–1564

We don't stop playing because
we grow old; we grow old
because we stop playing.

Geo Bernard Shaw

My dear child, you must believe in God in spite of what the clergy tell you.

Benjamin Jowett,
Anglican priest and scholar

My dear child, you must
believe in God in spite of
what the clergy tell you.

Benjamin Jowett,
Anglican priest and scholar

The only ones among you who will be truly happy are those who will have sought and found how to serve.

Albert Schweitzer

The rush and pressure of modern life are a form, perhaps the most common form, of contemporary violence. To allow oneself to be carried away by a multitude of conflicting concerns, to surrender to too many demands, to commit oneself to too many projects, to want to help everyone in everything is to succumb to violence.

Thomas Merton

The only ones among you who will be truly happy are those who will have sought and found how to serve.

Albert Schweitzer

The rush and pressure of modern life are a form, perhaps the most common form, of contemporary violence. To allow oneself to be carried away by a multitude of conflicting concerns, to surrender to too many demands, to commit oneself to too many projects, to want to help everyone in everything is to succumb to violence.

Thomas Merton

God does not die on the day when we cease to believe in a personal deity, but we die on the day when our lives cease to be illuminated by the steady radiance . . . the source of which is beyond reason.

Dag Hammarskjöld

All faith is experiment, and you cannot have the result of an experiment unless you make the experiment.

William Temple

It is permissible to pray for whatever it is permissible to desire.

Thos Aquinas

God does not die on the day
when we cease to believe in a
personal deity, but we die on
the day when our lives cease
to be illuminated by the steady
radiance . . . the source of
which is beyond reason.

Dag Hammarskjöld

All faith is experiment, and you
cannot have the result of an
experiment unless you make
the experiment.

William Temple

It is permissible to pray for
whatever it is permissible to desire.

Thos Aquinas

Because you are my help, I sing in the shadow of your wings.

Ps 63:7

Delight yourself in the Lord and he will give you the desires of your heart.

Ps 37:4

But those who hope in the Lord will renew their strength. They will soar on wings like eagles, they will run and not grow weary, they will walk and not be faint.

Isaiah 40:31

Because you are my help, I sing
in the shadow of your wings.

Ps 63:7

Delight yourself in the Lord
and he will give you the desires
of your heart.

Ps 37:4

But those who hope in the
Lord will renew their strength.
They will soar on wings like
eagles, they will run and not
grow weary, they will walk and
not be faint.

Isaiah 40:31

At times God puts us through the discipline of darkness to teach us to heed Him. Song birds are taught to sing in the dark, and we are put into the shadow of God's hand until we learn to hear Him . . . Are you in the dark just now in your circumstances, or in your life with God?

. . . When you are in the dark, listen, and God will give you a very precious message for someone else when you get into the light.

Oswald Chambers, *Utmost*,
reading for Feb 14

At times God puts us through
the discipline of darkness to
teach us to heed Him. Song
birds are taught to sing in the
dark, and we are put into the
shadow of God's hand until
we learn to hear Him . . .
Are you in the dark just now
in your circumstances, or in
your life with God?

. . . When you are in the dark,
listen, and God will give you
a very precious message for
someone else when you get into
the light.

Oswald Chambers, _Utmost,_
reading for Feb 14

Therefore encourage one another and build each other up.

1 Thessalonians 5:11

Taste and see that the Lord is good; blessed is the man who takes refuge in him.

Ps 34:8

For lo, the winter is past, the rain is over and gone. The flowers appear on the earth, the time of singing has come.

Song of Solomon 2:11–12

Therefore encourage one another
and build each other up.

> 1 Thessalonians 5:11

Taste and see that the Lord is
good; blessed is the man who
takes refuge in him.

> Ps 34:8

For lo, the winter is past, the
rain is over and gone. The
flowers appear on the earth,
the time of singing has come.

> Song of Solomon 2:11—12

When upon life's billows you are tempest tossed,
When you are discouraged, thinking all is lost,
Count your many blessings, name them one by one,
And *it will surprise you what the Lord hath done.*

—Johnson Oatman, old hymn

The Lord will guide you always, he will satisfy your needs in a sun-scorched land and will strengthen your frame. You will be like a well-watered garden, like a spring whose waters never fail.

Isaiah 58:11

When upon life's billows you are
        tempest tossed,
When you are discouraged,
        thinking all is lost,
Count your many blessings,
        name them one by one,
And it will surprise you
        what the Lord hath done.

        —Johnson Oatman, old hymn

The Lord will guide you always,
he will satisfy your needs in a
sun-scorched land and will
strengthen your frame. You
will be like a well-watered
garden, like a spring whose
waters never fail.

                Isaiah 58:11

". . . all things are possible with God."

Mark 10:27

"The Lord your God is with you, he is mighty to save. He will take great delight in you, he will quiet you with his love, he will rejoice over you with singing."

Zephaniah 3:17

God sings!! Remind choir

" . . . all things are possible with God."

Mark 10:27

"The Lord your God is with you, he is mighty to save. He will take great delight in you, he will quiet you with his love, he will rejoice over you with singing."

Zephaniah 3:17

God sings!! Remind choir

Scripture references re:
Barnabas:
Acts 4:36–37
Acts 9:26–27
Acts 11:22–25
Acts 11:20–30
Acts 13:2
13:43–48
14:13–18
14:20
15:2–11
15:22
15:37–40
Galatians 2:6–10
2:13

Scripture references re:

Barnabas:

Acts 4:36–37
Acts 9:26–27
Acts 11:22–25
Acts 11:20–30
Acts 13:2
13:43–48
14:13–18
14:20
15:2–11
15:22
15:37–40
Galatians 2:6–10
2:13

The next time you think you have an excuse why God can't use you, consider the following:

Noah was a drunkard, Abraham was too old, Isaac was a daydreamer, Jacob was a liar, Leah was ugly, Joseph was abused, Moses was a murderer, Gideon was afraid, Samson had long hair, Rahab was a prostitute, Timothy was too young, David had an illicit affair, Elijah was suicidal, Isaiah preached naked, Job was bankrupt, John the Baptist ran around in a loin

The next time you think you have an excuse why God can't use you, consider the following:

Noah was a drunkard, Abraham was too old, Isaac was a daydreamer, Jacob was a liar, Leah was ugly, Joseph was abused, Moses was a murderer, Gideon was afraid, Samson had long hair, Rahab was a prostitute, Timothy was too young, David had an illicit affair, Elijah was suicidal, Isaiah preached naked, Job was bankrupt, John the Baptist ran around in a loin—

cloth and ate locusts, Peter was hot-tempered, John was self-righteous.
The disciples fell asleep while praying, Martha fretted about everything, Mary Magadalene was demon-possessed, the boy with the fish and five rolls of bread was too obscure, the Samaritan woman was divorced more than once, Zacchaeus was too small, Paul was too religious, and Lazarus was dead.

No more excuses!

Author unknown

copy to Stuart,
Fr Roland

cloth and ate locusts, Peter was
hot-tempered, John was
self-righteous. The disciples fell
asleep while praying, Martha
fretted about everything,
Mary Magdalene was demon-
possessed, the boy with the fish
and five rolls of bread was too
obscure, the Samaritan woman
was divorced more than once,
Zacchaeus was too small,
Paul was too religious, and
Lazarus was dead.

No more excuses!

Author unknown

copy to Stuart,
Fr Roland

That which is . . . beautiful is not always good, but that which is good is always beautiful.

Ninon de L'Enclos

The heights by great men reached and
    kept
Were not attained by sudden flight,
But they, while their companions slept,
Were toiling upward in the night.

Longfellow, 1807–1882

It is wonderful what may be done if we are always doing.

Thos Jefferson

That which is . . . beautiful
is not always good, but that
which is good is always
beautiful.

Ninon de L'Enclos

The heights by great men reached
        and kept
Were not attained by sudden flight,
But they, while their companions
        slept,
Were toiling upward in the night.

Longfellow, 1807–1882

It is wonderful what may be
done if we are always doing.

Thos Jefferson

Overnight success takes a long time.

Stephen Jobs

There is no personal charm so great as the charm of a cheerful temperament.

Henry Van Dyke

A merry heart doeth good like a medicine.

Prov 17:22 KJV

Start by doing what's necessary, then what's possible, and suddenly, you are doing the impossible.

St Francis of Assisi

Overnight success takes a long time.

Stephen Jobs

There is no personal charm so great as the charm of a cheerful temperament.

Henry Van Dyke

A merry heart doeth good like a medicine.

Prov 17:22 KJV

Start by doing what's necessary, then what's possible, and suddenly, you are doing the impossible.

St Francis of Assisi

I never knew how to worship until I knew how to love.

Henry Ward Beecher

We are always planning to live . . .

Proust?

We are never living, but hoping to live.

Pascal

We are always getting ready to live, but never living.

Emerson

I never knew how to worship
until I knew how to love.

> Henry Ward Beecher

We are always planning
to live . . .

> Proust?

We are never living, but hoping
to live.

> Pascal

We are always getting ready to
live, but never living.

> Emerson

One of the most tragic things I know about human nature is that all of us tend to put off living. We are all dreaming of some magical rose garden over the horizon— instead of enjoying the roses that (bloom) outside our windows today.

Dale Carnegie

Do the ordinary things in an extraordinary way.

Geo. Allen, head coach
LA Rams, Wash. Redskins

One of the most tragic things
I know about human nature
is that all of us tend to put off
living. We are all dreaming of
some magical rose garden over
the horizon — instead of enjoying
the roses that (bloom) outside
our windows today.

Dale Carnegie

Do the ordinary things in an
extraordinary way.

Geo. Allen, head coach
LA Rams, Wash. Redskins

The true end of education is
Not only to make the young learned,
But to make them love learning,
Not only to make them industrious
But to make them love industry
Not only to make them virtuous,
But to make them love virtue . . .
Not only to make them just,
But to make them hunger and thirst after
   justice.

—The poet, John Ruskin,
who founded several schools

The true end of education is
Not only to make the young
          learned,
But to make them love learning,
Not only to make them
          industrious
But to make them love industry
Not only to make them virtuous,
But to make them love virtue . . .
Not only to make them just,
But to make them hunger and
          thirst after justice.

— The poet, John Ruskin,
   who founded several schools

Whether you think you can or you can't, you're absolutely right.

Henry Ford

Copy to Dooley

I think all Christians would agree with me if I said that though Christianity seems at first to be all about morality, all about duties and rules and guilt and virtue, yet it leads you on, out of all that, into something beyond.

CS Lewis, *Into Something Beyond*
August 18, St. Mark's, Lewisburg

Whether you think you can or
you can't, you're absolutely
right.

                    Henry Ford   Copy
                                        to
                                      Dooley.

I think all Christians would
 agree with me if I said that
though Christianity seems at
first to be all about morality, all
about duties and rules and guilt
and virtue, yet it leads you on,
out of all that, into something
beyond.

        CS Lewis, Into Something Beyond
            August 18, St. Mark's, Lewisburg

Richer than I you can never be
I had a mother who read to me.

Strickland Gillilan (Sp?)

A book that furnishes no quotations is, *me judice*, no book—it is a plaything.

Thomas Love Peacock

In our religious striving, we are usually looking for something quite other than the God who has come looking for us.

Eugene Peterson

Richer than I you can never be
I had a mother who read to me.
                    Strickland Gillilan (Sp?)

A book that furnishes no
quotations is, me judice, no book—
it is a plaything.
                    Thomas Love Peacock

In our religious striving, we are
usually looking for something
quite other than the God who
has come looking for us.
                    Eugene Peterson

"One Game At A Time," Rotary talk, Feb.

You've got to take it one game at a time, one hitter at a time. You've got to go on doing the things you've talked about and agreed about beforehand. You can't get three outs at a time or five runs at a time. You've got to concentrate on each play, each hitter, each pitch. All this makes the game much slower and much clearer. It breaks it down to its smallest part. If you take the game like that—one pitch, one hitter, one inning at a time, and then one game at a time—the next thing you know, you look up and you've won.

Rick Dempsey, baseball catcher.

Send to Stuart, Buck, Fr Roland

You've got to take it one game at a time, one hitter at a time. You've got to go on doing the things you've talked about and agreed about beforehand. You can't get three outs at a time or five runs at a time. You've got to concentrate on each play, each hitter, each pitch. All this makes the game much slower and much clearer. It breaks it down to its smallest part. If you take the game like that— one pitch, one hitter, one inning at a time, and then one game at a time— the next thing you know, you look up and you've won.

Rick Dempsey, baseball catcher.

Send to Stuart, Buck, Fr. Roland

"One Game At A Time, Rotary talk, Feb.

Dear God, be good to me, the sea is so wide and my boat is so small.

Prayer of Breton Fishermen

2/16 Am beginning the essays

Dear God, be good to me,
the sea is so wide
and my boat is so small.

Prayer of Breton Fishermen

2/16 Am beginning the essays

Just as the loaves increased when they were broken, the Lord has granted those things necessary to the beginning of this work, and when they (are) given out, they will be multiplied by His inspiration, so that in this task of mine I shall not only suffer no poverty of ideas but shall rejoice in wonderful abundance.

—St. Augustine

Just as the loaves increased
when they were broken, the
Lord has granted those things
necessary to the beginning of
this work, and when they (are)
given out, they will be multiplied by His inspiration,
so that in this task of mine
I shall not only suffer no
poverty of ideas but shall
rejoice in wonderful abundance.

   --St. Augustine

Essay fodder

"I'm not just a suit. I want the poetry back in my life."

Gerald Levin, upon his retirement
as CEO Time Warner

Sam. Johnson, 1709–1784:

The chains of habit are too weak to be felt until they are too strong to be broken.

Essay fodder

"I'm not just a suit. I want the poetry back in my life."

Gerald Levin, upon his retirement as CEO Time Warner

Sam. Johnson, 1709–1784:

The chains of habit are too weak to be felt until they are too strong to be broken.

Man's chief end is to glorify God and to enjoy Him forever.

Westminster Shorter Catechism

Pray as you can and do not try to pray as you can't.

John Chapman,
Eng. Benedictine monk

It is always springtime in the heart that loves God.

Jean-Baptiste-Marie Vianney,
Fr priest, 1786–1859

Man's chief end is to glorify
God and to enjoy Him forever.

Westminster Shorter Catechism

Pray as you can, and do not
try to pray as you can't.

John Chapman,
Eng. Benedictine monk

It is always springtime in the
heart that loves God.

Jean-Baptiste-Marie Vianney,
Fr. priest, 1786–1859

Moses dialogues with God, hammers
down, gets into relationship with the
Almighty:

. . . Oh! Teach us to live well!
Teach us to live wisely and well!
. . . Surprise us with love at daybreak:
Then we'll skip and dance all the day long.
Make up for the bad times with some good
    times;
We've seen enough evil to last a lifetime.
Let your servants see what you're best
    at—

Moses dialogues with God,
hammers down, gets into
relationship with the Almighty:

. . . Oh! Teach us to live well!
Teach us to live wisely and well!
. . . Surprise us with love at
daybreak.
Then we'll skip and dance all the
day long.
Make up for the bad times with
some good times;
We've seen enough evil to last a
lifetime.
Let your servants see what
you're best at—

The ways you rule and bless your children.
And let the loveliness of our Lord, our God, rest
On us,
Confirming the work that we do.
Oh, yes. Affirm the work that we do.

Eugene Peterson's translation
the 90th psalm, The Message

Where Christ is, cheerfulness will keep breaking in.

Dorothy Sayers

The ways you rule and bless
        your children.
And let the loveliness of our Lord,
        our God, rest
On us,
Confirming the work that we do.
Oh, yes. Affirm the work that
        we do.

                Eugene Peterson's translation
                the 90th psalm, The Message

Where Christ is, cheerfulness will
keep breaking in.

                        Dorothy Sayers

A sharp tongue is the only edged tool that grows keener with constant use.

Washington Irving

Whoso keepeth his mouth and his tongue keepeth his soul from troubles.

Prov 21:33

This

By long forbearing is a prince persuaded, and a soft tongue breaketh the bone.

Prov 25:15 KJV

A sharp tongue is the only
edged tool that grows keener
with constant use.

Washington Irving

Whoso keepeth his mouth and
his tongue keepeth his soul from
troubles.

Prov. 21:33

This

By long forbearing is a prince
persuaded, and a soft tongue
breaketh the bone.

Prov 25:15 KJV

A soft answer turneth away wrath . . .

Prov 15:1

The heart of the wise teacheth his mouth, and addeth learning to his lips.

Prov 16:23

Pleasant words are as an honeycomb, sweet to the soul, and health to the bones.

24

Correct thy son and he shall give thee rest; yea, he shall give delight unto thy soul.

Prov 29:17

A soft answer turneth away
wrath . . .
Prov 15:1

The heart of the wise teacheth
his mouth, and addeth
learning to his lips.
Prov 16:23

Pleasant words are as an
honeycomb, sweet to the soul,
and health to the bones.
24

Correct thy son and he shall
give thee rest; yea, he shall give
delight unto thy soul.
Prov 29:17

How much the wife is dearer than the bride.

George, Lord Lyttelton

You should always go to other people's funerals, otherwise they won't come to yours.

Yogi Berra

Human nature is what we were put on this earth to rise above.

K. Hepburn in *The African Queen*

How much the wife is dearer
than the bride.

George, Lord Lyttelton

You should always go to other
people's funerals, otherwise they
won't come to yours.

Yogi Berra

Human nature is what
we were put on this earth
to rise above.

K. Hepburn in *The African Queen*

We have all had times on the mount when we have seen things from God's standpoint and have wanted to stay there; but God will never allow us to stay there. The test of our spiritual life is the power to descend; if we have power to rise only, something is wrong.

—Oswald Chambers,
My Utmost,
reading for Oct 1

We have all had times on the
mount when we have seen thiings
from God's standpoint and have
wanted to stay there; but God
will never allow us to stay
there. The test of our spiritual liife is the power to
descend; if we have power to
riise only, something is wrong.

    --Oswald Chambers,
      ~~My~~ Utmost
      reading for Oct 1

We are not built for the mountains and the dawns and aesthetic affinities, those are for moments of inspiration, that is all. We are built for the valley, for the ordinary stuff we are in, and that is where we have to prove our mettle . . . The mount is not meant to teach us anything, it is meant to make us something.

—Ibid.

We are not built for the
mountaiins and the dawns and
aesthetic affinities, those are
for moments of inspiiration, that
is all. We are built for the
valley, for the ordinary stuff we
are in, and that is where we have
to prove our mettle . . . The
mount iis not meant to teach us
anything, it is meant to make
us something.

   --Ibiid.

If we are going to be made into wine, we will have to be crushed; you cannot drink grapes.

Ibid., Sept. 30

The very cream of Chambers

If we are going to be made
into wine, we will have to be
crushed; you cannot drink
grapes.

Ibid., Sept. 30

The very cream of Chambers

The preaching of the gospel awakens an intense resentment because it must reveal that I am unholy; but it also awakens an intense craving.

Ibid., Sept 1

Unless in the first waking moment of the day you learn to fling the door wide back and let God in, you will work on a wrong level all day; but swing the door wide . . . and pray to your Father . . . and every public thing will be stamped with the presence of God.

Ibid., Aug 23

No enthusiasm will ever stand the strain that Jesus Christ will put upon His worker, only one thing will, and that is a personal

The preaching of the gospel
awakens an intense resentment
because it must reveal that I am
unholy; but it also awakens an
intense craving.

Ibid., Sept 1

Unless in the first waking moment
of the day you learn to fling the
door wide back and let God in,
you will work on a wrong level all
day; but swing the door wide . . .
and pray to your Father . . . and
every public thing will be stamped
with the presence of God.

Ibid., Aug 23

No enthusiasm will ever stand the
strain that Jesus Christ will put
upon His worker, only one thing
will, and that is a personal

relationship to Himself which has gone through the mill of His spring-cleaning . . .

Ibid., Sept 25

We have to take the first step as though there were no God. It is no use to wait for God to help us, He will not; but immediately we arise we find He is there . . .

Ibid., Feb 19

Let the past sleep, but let it sleep on the bosom of Christ, and go out into the irresistible future with Him.

Ibid., Feb 17

The Irresistible Future, March 17, St. Paul's

relationship to Himself which
has gone through the mill of
His spring-cleaning. . .

Ibid., Sept 25

We have to take the first step as
though there were no God. It is
no use to wait for God to help us,
He will not; but immediately we
arise we find He is there. . .

Ibid., Feb 19

Let the past sleep, but let it sleep on
the bosom of Christ, and go out
into the irresistible future with Him.

Ibid., Feb 17

The
Irresistible
Future,
March 17,
St. Paul's

On Giving

. . . give, and it will be given unto you.

Luke 6:38

He that hath a bountiful eye shall be blessed; for he giveth of his bread to the poor.

Proverbs 22:9

We are not cisterns made for hoarding; we are channels made for giving.

Billy Graham

Giving is the secret of a healthy life . . . not necessarily money, but whatever a man has of encouragement and sympathy and understanding.

John D. Rockefeller, Jr.

On Giving

. . . give, and it will be given
unto you.

Luke 6:38

He that hath a bountiful eye
shall be blessed; for he giveth of
his bread to the poor.

Proverbs 22:9

We are not cisterns made for
hoarding; we are channels
made for giving.

Billy Graham

Giving is the secret of a healthy
life . . . not necessarily money,
but whatever a man has of
encouragement and sympathy
and understanding.

John D. Rockefeller, Jr.

I never look at the masses as my responsibility. I look at the individual. I can only love one person at a time.

Mother Teresa

Philanthropy from the Greek *philanthropos*, or lover of mankind

As Christians, we can't love the whole world. But we should remember that God has placed us in a specific community at a particular time. We're called to love those around us. Loving them means serving them—and in doing so, we become the best of citizens.

C.S. Lewis

I never look at the masses as my responsibility. I look at the individual. I can only love one person at a time.

Mother Teresa

Philanthropy from the Greek philanthropos, or lover of mankind

As Christians, we can't love the whole world. But we should remember that God has placed us in a specific community at a particular time. We're called to love those around us. Loving them means serving them — and in doing so, we become the best of citizens.

C.S. Lewis

For several centuries
famous birds have flown over
the vast fields of poetry

the swallow the nightingale the lark
the skylark the linnet the
    hummingbird
the raven the golden oriole
and of course the phoenix
have all been invited by poets
to populate their forests
decorate their skies
and stuff their metaphors

I'm going to stick my neck out here
for the discriminated birds /
    those that never
or only rarely make an appearance
those poor forgotten birds
that are full of memory

For several centuries
famous birds have flown over
the vast fields of poetry

the swallow the nightingale the lark
the skylark the linnet the
        hummingbird
the raven the golden oriole
and of course the phoenix
have all been invited by poets
to populate their forests
decorate their skies
and stuff their metaphors

I'm going to stick my neck out here
for the discriminated birds / those
        that never
or only rarely make an appearance
those poor forgotten birds
that are full of memory

Ask Hope, C's b'day

and so here I write
the canary the sparrow the thrush
　　the blackbird
the widow the starling the cardinal
the turtledove the magpie the
　　gardener
the kingfisher the king-bird
so that they can make their way
　　into poetry at least
this once
even it it's just / as on this occasion
through the back door.

"Birds," by Mario Benedetti,
         transl. from the Spanish by Charles
            Hatfield, from *Little Stones at my
                   Window* by Benedetti

Ask Hope, C's b'day

and so here I write
the canary the sparrow the thrush
        the blackbird
the widow the starling the cardinal
the turtledove the magpie the
            gardener
the kingfisher the king—bird
so that they can make their way
        into poetry at least
this once
even if it's just / as on this occasion
through the back door.

        "Birds," by Mario Benedetti,
    transl. from the Spanish by Charles
    Hatfield, from _Little Stones at my_
                Window by Benedetti

Copy for C:

Be like the bird
That, pausing in her flight
Awhile on boughs too slight,
Feels them give way
Beneath her and yet sings,
Knowing that she hath wings.

Victor Hugo

Copy for C:

Be like the bird
That, pausing in her flight
Awhile on boughs too slight,
Feels them give way
Beneath her and yet sings,
Knowing that she hath wings.

                                  Victor Hugo

Through the call of Jesus men become individuals. Willy-nilly, they are compelled to decide, and that decision can only be made by themselves. It is no choice of their own that makes them individuals: it is Christ who makes them individuals by calling them. *Every man is called separately, and must follow alone.*

Bonhoeffer, The Cost of Discipleship

Through the call of Jesus men become individuals. Willy-nilly, they are compelled to decide, and that decision can only be made by themselves. It is no choice of their own that makes them individuals: it is Christ who makes them individuals by calling them. _Every man is called separately, and must follow alone._

Bonhoeffer, The Cost of Discipleship

You have not chosen me but I have chosen you, and ordained you, that you should go and bring forth fruit and that your fruit should remain.

St. John 14:15–16

Remembering
  His call . . .
Holly Springs,
    July 28 . . .

In daily life we must see that it is not happiness that makes us grateful, but gratefulness that makes us happy.

Unknown

Yes!

You have not chosen me but I have chosen you, and ordained you, that you should go and bring forth fruit and that your fruit should remain.

St. John 14:15—16

HOLLY
SPRINGS

Remembering
His call . . .
Holly Springs,
July 28 . . .

In daily life we must see that it is not happiness that makes us grateful, but gratefulness that makes us happy.

Unknown

Yes!

You must plough with such oxen as you
have.

Again, yes!

What do we live for, if not to make the
world less difficult for each other?

George Eliot

Carry each other's burdens, and in this
way you will fulfill the law of Christ.

Galatians 6:2, NIV

Above all, love each other deeply, because
love covers over a multitude of sins.

1 Peter 4:8 NIV

Love makes all hard hearts gentle.

George Herbert

You must plough with such
oxen as you have.
English proverb

Again, Yes!

What do we live for, if not to
make the world less difficult for
each other?
George Eliot

Carry each other's burdens, and
in this way you will fulfill the
law of Christ.
Galatians 6:2, NIV

Above all, love each other deeply,
because love covers over a
multitude of sins.
1 Peter 4:8 NIV

Love makes all hard hearts
gentle.
George Herbert

Lord I know not what to ask of Thee; Thou knowest what I need; Thou lovest me better than I know how to love myself. O Father, give to Thy child that which he himself knows not how to ask. I dare not ask either for crosses or for consolations; I simply present myself before Thee. I open my heart to Thee. Behold my needs which I know not myself; see and do according to Thy tender mercy . . .

François de Salignac Fénelon,
1651–1751

Lord I know not what to ask
of Thee; Thou knowest what I
need; Thou lovest me better than
I know how to love myself.
O Father, give to Thy child that
which he himself knows not
how to ask. I dare not ask either
for crosses or for consolations;
I simply present myself before Thee.
I open my heart to Thee. Behold
my needs which I know not
myself; see and do according to
Thy tender mercy . . .

François de Salignac Fénelon,
1651—1751

To live content with small means; to seek elegance rather than luxury, and refinement rather than fashion; to be worthy, not respectable, and wealthy, not rich; to listen to stars and birds, babes and sages, with open heart; to study hard; to think quietly, act frankly, talk gently, await occasions, hurry never; in a word, to let the spiritual, unbidden and unconscious, grow up through the common—this is my symphony.

William Henry Channing, clergyman, reformer, 1810–1884

'Tis the good reader that makes the good book.

Emerson

To live content with small means;
to seek elegance rather than luxury,
and refinement rather than
fashion; to be worthy, not
respectable, and wealthy, not rich;
to listen to stars and birds, babes
and sages, with open heart; to
study hard; to think quietly, act
frankly, talk gently, await
occasions, hurry never; in a word,
to let the spiritual, unbidden and
unconscious, grow up through
the common—this is my
symphony.

William Henry Channing, clergyman,
reformer, 1810—1884

'Tis the good reader that makes
the good book.

Emerson

What is this life if, full of care,
We have no time to stand and
  stare?—
No time to stand beneath the
  boughs
And stare as long as sheep or cows:
No time to see, when woods we
  pass,
Where squirrels hide their nuts in
  grass:
No time to see, in broad daylight,
Streams full of stars, like skies at
  night:
No time to turn at Beauty's
  glance,
And watch her feet, how they
  can dance:
No time to wait till her mouth
  can

What is this life if, full of care,
We have no time to stand and
              stare? —
No time to stand beneath the
              boughs
And stare as long as sheep or cows:
No time to see, when woods we
              pass,
Where squirrels hide their nuts in
              grass:
No time to see, in broad daylight,
Streams full of stars, like skies at
              night:
No time to turn at Beauty's
              glance,
And watch her feet, how they
              can dance:
No time to wait till her mouth
              can

Enrich that smile her eyes began?
A poor life this if, full of care,
We have no time to stand and stare.

William Henry Davies, b. 1871

Reading yet again in the Quiller-Couch
edition, Oxford Bk Eng Verse 4/17

I am not a has-been. I am a will-be.

Lauren Bacall

Enrich that smile her eyes began?
A poor life this if, full of care,
We have no time to stand and
    stare.
William Henry Davies, b. 1871

Reading yet again in the Quiller—
Couch edition, Oxford Bk Eng
Verse 4/17

I am not a has—been.
I am a will—be.
    Lauren Bacall

Knowledge comes, but wisdom lingers.

Tennyson

A man's language is an unerring index of his nature.

Laurence Binyon

Wisdom!
I make the most of all that comes,
And the least of all that goes.

Sara Teasdale

Laughter is the sun that drives winter from the human face.

Victor Hugo

Our bodies are our gardens, to which our wills are gardeners.

Shakespeare

Selah!

Knowledge comes, but wisdom
lingers.

                           Tennyson

A man's language is an
unerring index of his nature.

                         Laurence Binyon

I make the most of all that
Wisdom!   comes,
And the least of all that goes.

                         Sara Teasdale

Laughter is the sun that drives
winter from the human face.

                         Victor Hugo

Our bodies are our gardens, to
which our wills are gardeners.

Selah!   Shakespeare

Directions for Singing

I. Learn these tunes before you learn any others; afterwards learn as many as you please.

II. Sing them exactly as they are printed here, without altering or mending them at all; and if you have learned to sing them otherwise, unlearn it as soon as you can.

III. Sing all. See that you join with the congregation as frequently as you can. Let not a slight degree of weakness or weariness hinder you. If it is a cross to you, take it up, and you will find it a blessing.

Directions for Singing

I. Learn these tunes before you
learn any others; afterwards learn
as many as you please.

II. Sing them exactly as they are
priinted here, without altering
or mending them at all; and iif
you have learned to sing them
otherwise, unlearn it as soon
as you can.

III. ⌀ Sing all. See that you join
with the congregation as frequently
as you can. Lot not a sliight
degree of weakness or weariness
hiinder you. If it is a cross to
you, take it up, and you wiill
find it a blessing.

IV. Sing lustily and with a good courage. Beware of singing as if you were half dead, or half asleep; but lift up your voice with strength. Be no more afraid of your voice now, nor more ashamed of its being heard, than when you sang the songs of Satan.

V. Sing modestly. Do not bawl, so as to be heard above or distinct from the rest of the congregation, that you may not destroy the harmony; but strive to unite your voices together, so as to make one clear melodious sound.

IV. Sing lustily and with a good
courage. Beware of singing as iif
you were half dead, or half
asleep; but lift up your voice
with strength. Be no more afraiid
of your voice now, nor more
ashamed of its being heard, than
when you sang the songs of Satan.
V. Sing modestly. Do not bawl, so
as to be heard above or distinct
from the rest of the congregatiion,
that you may not destroy the harmony; but strive to unite your v
voices together, so as to make one
clear melodiious sound.

VI. Sing in time. Whatever time is sung be sure to keep with it. Do not run before nor stay behind it; but attend close to the leading voices, and move therewith as exactly as you can; and take care not to sing too slow. This dawdling way naturally steals on all who are lazy; and it is high time to drive it out from us, and sing all our tunes just as quick as we did at first.

VII. Above all sing spiritually. Have an eye to God in every word you sing. Aim at pleasing him more than yourself, or any other creature. In order to do this attend

VI. Sing in time. Whatever time
is sung be sure to keep with it.
Do not run before nor stay behind it; but attend close to the
leading voices, and move there-
wiith as exactly as you can; and
take care not to sing too slow.
This dawdling way naturally
steals on all who are lazy; and
it is hiigh time to drive it out
from us, and sing all our tunes
just as quick as we did at first.
VII. Above all sing spiritually.
Have an eye to God in every word
you sing. Aim at pleasing him more
thank yourself, or any other creature. In order to do thiis attend

strictly to the sense of what you sing, and see that your heart is not carried away with the sound, but offered to God continually; so shall your singing be such as the Lord will approve here, and reward you when he cometh in the clouds of heaven.

—From John Wesley's preface to
Sacred Melody, 1761

So absolutely good is truth, truth never hurts the teller.

Robert Browning

strictly to the sense of what
you sing, and see that your
heart is not carriied away with
the sound, but offered to God
continually; so shall your
singiing be such as the Lord
will apprve here, and reward
you when he cometh in the clouds
of heaven.

  --From John Wesley's preface to
    Sacred Melody, 1761

So absolutely good is truth,
truth never hurts the teller.

              Robert Browning

No one can be wrong with man and right with God.

Harry Emerson Fosdick Eph. 4:32

Most days I side with the French oddsmaker, Blaise Pascal, whose gambit instructs that it is better to believe in something that isn't than to disbelieve in something that is.

Thomas Lynch

When you accept the fact of God, you simultaneously admit your responsibility toward all creation. *There is no such thing as a private act.*

John Aurelio

No one can be wrong with man
and right with God.

Harry Emerson Fosdick Eph. 4:32

Most days I side with the
French oddsmaker, Blaise
Pascal, whose gambit instructs
that it is better to believe in
something that isn't than to
disbelieve in something that is.

Thomas Lynch

When you accept the fact of
God, you simultaneously
admit your responsibility
toward all creation. There is no
such thing as a private act.

John Aurelio

He said not:
Thou shalt not be troubled, thou shalt not
be tempted, thou shalt not be distressed,
but He said: thou shalt not be overcome.

Julian of Norwich

I am absolutely unshaken in my faith that
God created us, loves us, and wants us
not only to be good but to be happy.

Archibald Rutledge

There! What Lewis
was getting at —

He said not:
Thou shalt not be troubled,
thou shalt not be tempted, thou
shalt not be distressed, but
He said: thou shalt not be
overcome.

                          Julian of Norwich

I am absolutely unshaken in
my faith that God created us,
loves us, and wants us not
only to be good but to be happy.

                          Archibald Rutledge

There! What Lewis
was getting at—

There is a sense in which (God) is at the tip of my pen, my spade, my brush, my needle—of my heart and of my thoughts.

Teilhard de Chardin

Lord, as I scribe these essays, be faithfully at the tip of my heart, thoughts, and pen, I pray thee

Copy for C

There is a sense in which (God)
is at the tip of my pen, my
spade, my brush, my needle — of
my heart and of my thoughts.

Teilhard de Chardin

Lord, as I scribe these essays,
be faithfully at the tip of my
heart, thoughts, and pen,
I pray thee

Copy for C

Most people would sooner die than think; in fact, they do so.

Bertrand Russell

You and I are here to do good to others. What the others are here for, I don't know.

W. H. Auden

I will not give to the Lord that which costs me nothing.

II Samuel? Confirm this

Faith means believing the unbelievable, or it is no virtue at all.

G. K. Chesterton

Most people would sooner die
than think; in fact, they do so.

Bertrand Russell

You and I are here to do good
to others. What the others are
here for, I don't know.

W. H. Auden

I will not give to the Lord that
which costs me nothing.

II Samuel? Confirm this

Faith means believing the
unbelievable, or it is no virtue
at all.

G. K. Chesterton

You're as welcome as flowers in May.

> Charles Macklin
> My mother's old saying

If I were to wish for anything, I should not wish for wealth and power, but for the passionate sense of the potential, for the eye which, *ever young and ardent,* sees the possible.

> Kierkegaard

True elegance consists of saying all that should be said, and that only.

> François de La Rochefoucauld,
> 1613–1680

You're as welcome as flowers
in May.
      Charles Macklin
            My mother's old saying

If I were to wish for anything,
I should not wish for wealth
and power, but for the
passionate sense of the potential,
for the eye which, _ever young_
and ardent, sees the possible.

                        Kierkegaard

True elegance consists of saying
all that should be said, and
that only.
            François de La Rochefoucauld,
                        1613-1680

I can no answer make but thanks, and thanks, and ever thanks.

Shakespeare

Remember this—that very little is needed to make a happy life.

Marcus Aurelius

Plunge boldly into the thick of life.

Goethe (1749–1832)

Come boldly to the throne of grace . . .

Hebrews

Yielding to Jesus will break every form of slavery in any human life.

Oswald, Utmost

I can no answer make
but thanks, and thanks,
and ever thanks.

Shakespeare

Remember this— that very little is
needed to make a happy life.

Marcus Aurelius

Plunge boldly into the thick of life.

Goethe (1749—1832)

Come boldly to the throne of
grace . . .

Hebrews

Yielding to Jesus will break
every form of slavery in any
human life.

Oswald, Utmost

WHEN YOU CANNOT PRAY AS YOU WOULD, PRAY AS YOU CAN.

Dean Goulburn
Yes!

Every branch that does bear fruit, He prunes so that it will be even more fruitful.

Sermon 8/28

Our real blessings often appear to us in the shape of pains, losses and disappointments; but let us have patience and we shall soon see them in their proper figures.

Joseph Addison

Mark this well

WHEN YOU CANNOT PRAY AS YOU
WOULD, PRAY AS YOU CAN.

Dean Goulburn
Yes!

Every branch that does bear
fruit, He prunes so that it will
be even more fruitful.

Sermon 8/28

Our real blessings often appear
to us in the shape of pains,
losses and disappointments;
but let us have patience and
we shall soon see them in their
proper figures.

Joseph Addison

Mark this well

Listen, listen to me, and eat what is good, and your soul will delight in the richest of fare. Give ear and come to me; hear me, that your soul may live.

Isaiah 55:3

Listen, listen to me, and eat what is good, and your soul will delight in the richest of fare. Give ear and come to me; hear me, that your soul may live.

Isaiah 55:3

I am the good shepherd . . . I know my sheep.

John 10:14–15

I have called you by name—you are mine.

Isaiah 43:1

I will give you the treasures of darkness, riches stored in secret places, so that you may know that I am the Lord, the God of Israel, who summons you by name.

Isaiah 45:3

I am the good shepherd . . .
I know my sheep.

John 10:14—15

I have called you by name
you are mine.

Isaiah 43:1

I will give you the treasures of
darkness, riches stored in secret
places, so that you may know
that I am the Lord, the God
of Israel, who summons you
by name.

Isaiah 45:3

What a large volume of adventures may be grasped within this little span of life by him who interests his heart in everything.

Laurence Sterne

If a nation expects to be ignorant and free, it expects what never was and never will be.

Thos Jefferson

Storms make oaks take deeper root.

George Herbert

What a large volume of
adventures may be grasped
within this little span of life
by him who interests his heart
in everything.

Laurence Sterne

If a nation expects to be
ignorant and free, it expects
what never was and never
will be.

Thos Jefferson

Storms make oaks take deeper
root.

George Herbert

The problem with miracles is that it is hard to witness them without wanting one of your own.

Barbara Brown Taylor

Day by day we are given not what we want but what we need. Sometimes it is a feast and sometimes . . . swept crumbs, but by faith we believe it is enough.

BBT as above

The problem with miracles is
that it is hard to witness them
without wanting one of your
own.

                    Barbara Brown Taylor

Day by day we are given not
what we want but what we
need. Sometimes it is a feast and
sometimes . . . swept crumbs,
but by faith we believe it is
enough.

                    BBT as above

All men wonder to see water turned into wine. Every day the earth's moisture, being drawn into the . . . vine, is turned by the grape into wine, and no man wonders.

Gregory the Great

This

All men wonder to see water
turned into wine. Every day
the earth's moisture, being
drawn into the . . . vine, is
turned by the grape into wine,
and no man wonders.

                    Gregory the Great

This

Great works are performed not by strength but by perseverance.

Samuel Johnson

I can do all things through Christ who strengthens me.

Philippians 4:13

I haven't failed, I've just found 10,000 ways that won't work.

Thos Edison

Persistence can grind an iron beam down into a needle.

Chinese proverb

And the squeaking wheel gets the grease!

Great works are performed not
by strength but by perseverance.

Samuel Johnson

I can do all things through
Christ who strengthens me.

Philippians 4:13

I haven't failed, I've just
found 10,000 ways that
won't work.

Thos Edison

Persistence can grind an iron
beam down into a needle.

Chinese proverb

And the squeaking wheel gets the grease!

Why am I dosing you with these antediluvian topics? Because I am glad to have someone to whom they are familiar, and who will not receive them as if dropped from the moon.

Thos Jefferson

Send to Stuart, copy for C

Why am I dosing you with these antediluvian topics? Because I am glad to have someone to whom they are familiar, and who will not receive them as if dropped from the moon.

Thos Jefferson

Send to Stuart, copy for C

Emma's peach cobbler recipe:

1/2 cp butter
2 cups sugar, divided
4 cps sliced fresh peaches
1 cp self-rising flour
1 cp milk

Melt butter in a 13x9x2" pan. Combine flour, 1 cp sugar, and milk, mix well. Pour over melted butter, don't stir. Combine peaches and remaining cp sugar in a saucepan; bring to boil. Pour over batter, don't stir. Bake at 375 for 30 mins or until browned.

10 servings, 4 if Dooley is home.

Emma's peach cobbler recipe:

1/2 cp butter
2 cups sugar, divided
4 cps sliced fresh peaches
1 cp self-rising flour
1 cp milk

Melt butter in a 13 x 9 x 2" pan.
Combine flour, 1 cp sugar, and
milk, mix well. Pour over melted
butter, don't stir. Combine
peaches and remaining cp sugar
in a saucepan; bring to boil.
Pour over batter, don't stir.
Bake at 375 for 30 mins or
until browned.
10 servings, 4 if Dooley is home.

In general those who have nothing to say
Contrive to spend the longest time in doing
it.

James Russell Lowell

How often—will it be for always?—how
often will the vast emptiness astonish me
like a complete novelty and make me say,
"I never realized my loss till this moment"?

Lewis, A Grief Observed

More frequent visits to Louella

In general those who have
nothing to say
Contrive to spend the longest time
in doing it.

James Russell Lowell

How often—will it be for always?—
how often will the vast emptiness
astonish me like a complete
novelty and make me say, "I never
realized my loss till this moment"?

Lewis, A Grief Observed

More frequent visits to

Louella

One of the most attractive things about flowers is their beautiful reserve.

Thoreau

A thing constructed can only be loved after it is constructed, but a thing created is loved before it exists.

G. K. Chesterton

Divine implications!

A small drop of ink produces that which makes thousands think.

Lord Byron

That is happiness; to be dissolved into something complete and great.

Willa Cather

One of the most attractive things about flowers is their beautiful reserve.

Thoreau

A thing constructed can only be loved after it is constructed; but a thing created is loved before it exists.

G. K. Chesterton

Divine implications!

A small drop of ink produces that which makes thousands think.

Lord Byron

That is happiness; to be dissolved into something complete and great.

Willa Cather

The Possible's slow fuse is lit by the Imagination.

Emily Dickinson

One of the many things nobody ever tells you about middle age is that it's such a nice change from being young.

Dorothy Canfield Fisher

Work is not always required . . . there is such a thing as sacred idleness, the cultivation of which is now fearfully neglected.

George Macdonald

The Possible's slow fuse is lit by
the Imagination.

Emily Dickinson

One of the many things nobody
ever tells you about middle age is
that it's such a nice change
from being young.

Dorothy Canfield Fisher

Work is not always required . . .
there is such a thing as sacred
idleness, the cultivation of which
is now fearfully neglected.

George Macdonald

You have rescued me from death; you have kept my feet from slipping. So now I can walk in your presence, O God, in your life-giving light.

Psalm 56:13

The unfailing love of the Lord never ends. By his mercies we have been kept from complete destruction. Great is his faithfulness; his mercies begin afresh each day.

Lamentations 3:22–23

You have rescued me from death; you have kept my feet from slipping. So now I can walk in your presence, O God, in your life-giving light.

Psalm 56:13

The unfailing love of the Lord never ends. By his mercies we have been kept from complete destruction. Great is his faithfulness; his mercies begin afresh each day.

Lamentations 3:22—23

Dogs!
Anybody who doesn't know what soap
tastes like never washed a dog.

—Franklin P. Jones

"Dogs are our link to paradise. They don't
know evil or jealousy or discontent. To sit
with a dog on a hillside on a glorious
afternoon is to be back in Eden, where
doing nothing was not boring—it was
peace."

—Milan Kundera

Dogs never lie about love.

Jeffrey Masson

Dogs!
Anybody who doesn't know
what soap tastes like never
washed a dog.

— Franklin P. Jones

"Dogs are our link to paradise.
They don't know evil or jealousy
or discontent. To sit with a dog
on a hillside on a glorious
afternoon is to be back in Eden,
where doing nothing was not
boring — it was peace."

— Milan Kundera

Dogs never lie about love.

Jeffrey Masson

I care not for a man's religion whose dog and cat are not the better for it.

Abraham Lincoln

. . . people who keep dogs . . . are cowards who haven't got the guts to bite people themselves.

August Strindberg

A dog teaches a boy fidelity, perseverance, and to turn around three times before lying down.

Robert Benchley

Cat motto: No matter what you've done wrong, always try to make it look like the dog did it.

—Unknown

I care not for a man's religion
whose dog and cat are not the
better for it.

Abraham Lincoln

. . . people who keep dogs . . .
are cowards who haven't got
the guts to bite people themselves.

August Strindberg

A dog teaches a boy fidelity,
perseverance, and to turn around
three times before lying down.

Robert Benchley

Cat motto: No matter what
you've done wrong, always try
to make it look like the dog did it.

— Unknown

From the venerable wayside pulpit:

Worry about nothing.
Pray about everything.

Shorthand
for Philippians 4:6

from the venerable wayside
pulpit :

Worry about nothing.
Pray about everything.

Shorthand
for Philippians 4:6

Middle age is when you've met so many
people that every new person you meet
reminds you of someone else.

Ogden Nash

I seldom made an errand to God for
another, but I got something for myself.

Samuel Rutherford

Middle age is when you've met
so many people that every new
person you meet reminds you
of someone else.

Ogden Nash

I seldom made an errand to
God for another, but I got
something for myself.

Samuel Rutherford

From the last words of Thos Cranmer,
author 1549 BCP

All men desire . . . at the time of their
deaths, to give some good exhortation that
others may remember . . . and be the
better thereby

(from the Anglican Digest)

What might my own be?
Ask C hers

Nothing strengthens the judgment and
quickens the conscience like individual
responsibility.

Elizabeth Cady Stanton

from the last words of Thos
Cranmer, author 1549 BCP

All men desire . . . at the time
of their deaths, to give some
good exhortation that others
may remember . . . and be the
better thereby
                    (from the Anglican Digest)

What might my own be?
Ask Chers

        Nothing strengthens the
        judgment and quickens the
        conscience like individual
        responsibility.

                    Elizabeth Cady Stanton

God preserves his order despite our chaos.

Elizabeth Achtemeier

It is a general popular error to imagine the loudest complainers for the public to be the most anxious for its welfare.

Edmund Burke

Natural ability without education has more often raised a man to glory and virtue than education without natural ability.

Cicero

God preserves his order despite
our chaos.

Elizabeth Achtemeier

It is a general popular error to
imagine the loudest complainers
for the public to be the most
anxious for its welfare.

Edmund Burke

Natural ability without education
has more often raised a man to
glory and virtue than education
without natural ability.

Cicero

I cannot remember a time when I was not in love with them—with the books themselves, cover and binding and the paper they were printed on, with their smell and their weight and with their possession in my arms, captured and carried off to myself.

Eudora Welty

The expression of Christian character is not good doing, but God-likeness. God's life in us expresses itself as God's life, not as human life trying to be godly.

Osw. Chambers, Utmost, June 28

Not good doing, but God-likeness

I cannot remember a time when
I was not in love with them—
with the books themselves,
cover and binding and the
paper they were printed on,
with their smell and their
weight and with their possession
in my arms, captured and
carried off to myself.
                        Eudora Welty

The expression of Christian
character is not good doing, but
God-likeness. God's life in us
expresses itself as God's life, not
as human life trying to be godly.
        Osw. Chambers, Utmost, June 28

Not good doing, but God-likeness

The cream of enjoyment in this life is always impromptu. The chance walk; the unexpected visit; the unpremeditated journey; the unsought conversation or acquaintance.

Fanny Fern

Forty is the old age of youth; fifty is the youth of old age.

French proverb

. . . the world can forgive practically anything except people who mind their own business.

Margaret Mitchell

The cream of enjoyment in this life is always impromptu. The chance walk; the unexpected visit; the unpremeditated journey; the unsought conversation or acquaintance.

Fanny Fern

Forty is the old age of youth; fifty is the youth of old age.

French proverb

. . . the world can forgive practically anything except people who mind their own business.

Margaret Mitchell

Nothing shows a man's character more than what he laughs at.

Goethe

Success is not the key to happiness. Happiness is the key to success. If you love what you are doing, you will be successful.

A. Schweitzer

We all have to die someday, if we live long enough.

Dave Farber

Nothing shows a man's
character more than what
he laughs at.

Goethe

Success is not the key to
happiness. Happiness is the key
to success. If you love what
you are doing, you will be
successful.

A. Schweitzer

We all have to die someday,
if we live long enough.

Dave Farber

The newest books are those that never grow old.

George Holbrook Jackson

The worst thing about new books is that they keep us from reading the old ones.

Joseph Joubert

Everywhere I have sought rest and not found it, except sitting in a corner by myself with a little book.

Thomas à Kempis

copy
for HW

The newest books are those that
never grow old.

George Holbrook Jackson

The worst thing about new
books is that they keep us from
reading the old ones.

Joseph Joubert

Everywhere I have sought rest
and not found it, except sitting
in a corner by myself with a
little book.

Thomas à Kempis

Copy
for HW

The reading of July 6, from "Utmost"—the reading I admire above all others

"And the parched ground shall become a pool." Isaiah 35:7

We always have visions, before a thing is made real. When we realize that although the vision is real, it is not real in us, then is the time that Satan comes in with his temptations, and we are apt to say that it is no use to go on. Instead of the vision becoming real, there has come the valley of humiliation.

"Life is not as idle ore,
But iron dug from central gloom,
And batter'd by the shocks of doom
To shape and use."

God gives us the vision, then He takes us down to the valley to batter us into the shape of the vision, and it is in the valley that so many of us faint and give way. Every vision will be made real if we will have patience. Think of the enormous leisure of God! He is never in a hurry. We are always

The reading of July 6, from "Utmost"--
   the reading I admire above all
   others

"And the parched ground shall become a pool." Isaiah 35:7

We always have visions, before a
thing is made real. When we realize that although the vision is
real, it is not real in us, then
is the time that Satan comes in
with his temptations, and we are
apt to say that is is no use to
go on. Instead of the vision becoming real, there has come the
valley of humiiliation.

"Life is not as idle ore,
But iron dug from central gloom,
And batter'd by the shocks of doom,
To shape and use."

God gives us the vision, then He
takes us down to the valley to
batter us into the shape of the
vision, and it is in the valley
that so many of us faint and
give way. Every vision will be made
real if we will have patience. Think
of the enormous leisure of God! He
is never in a hurry. We are always

in such a frantic hurry. In the light of the glory of the vision we go forth to do things, but the vision is not real in us yet; and God has to take us into the valley, and put us through fires and floods to batter us into shape, until we get to the place where He can trust us with the veritable reality. Ever since we had the vision God has been at work, getting us into the shape of the ideal, and over and over again we escape from His hand and try to batter ourselves into our own shape.

The vision is not a castle in the air, but a vision of what God wants you to be. Let Him put you on His wheel and whirl you as He likes, and as sure as God is God and you are you, you will turn out exactly in accordance with the vision. Don't lose heart in the process. If you have ever had the vision of God, you may try as you like to be satisfied on a lower level, but God will never let you.

in such a frantic hurry. In the
light of the glory of the vision
we go forth to do things, but the
vision is not real in us yet; and
God has to take us into the valley,
and put us through fires and
floods to batter us into shape,
until we get to the place where
He can trust us with the veriitable
reality. Ever since we had the
vision God has been at work, getting us into the shape of the
ideal, and over and over again we
escape from His hand and try to
batter ourselves into our own
shape.

The vision is not a castle in
the air, but a vision of what
God wants you to be. Let Him
put you on His wheel and whirl
you as He likes, and as sure
as God is God and you are you,
you will turn out exactly in
accordance with the vision. Don´t
lose heart in the process. If
you have ever had the vision of
God, you may try as you like to
be satisfied on a lower level,
but God wiill never let you.

On bereavement:

It is not that we feel cut off from the bigger spiritual relationship which survives death, but from the hundred and one lesser links which bind people together, incidental things which when looked back on seem of enduring significance, but which were taken so much for granted at the time. The other person's sense of humor, prejudices, moods, all that has gone. For the rest of our lives we shall have to do without his mannerisms, his shyness, his ways of pronouncing things.

On bereavement:

It is not that we feel cut off
from the bigger spiritual
relationship which survives
death, but from the hundred
and one lesser links which bind
people together, incidental things
which when looked back on
seem of enduring significance,
but which were taken so much
for granted at the time. The
other person's sense of humor,
prejudices, moods, all that has
gone. For the rest of our lives we
shall have to do without his
mannerisms, his shyness, his
ways of pronouncing things.

The voice is silent—we had expected it would be—but that the yawns and burst of laughter will never be repeated is almost more than we can bear . . . Those moments were not passing moments at all. *They had something in them of eternity* . . .

Hubert van Zeller, Moments of Light,
Springfield, Ill., Template, 1963

The voice is silent— we had
expected it would be — but that
the yawns and bursts of laughter
will never be repeated is almost
more than we can bear . . .
Those moments were not passing
moments at all. They had
something in them of eternity . . .

Hubert van Zeller, Moments of Light,
Springfield, Ill., Template, 1963

Most of the important things in the world have been accomplished by people who have kept on trying when there seemed to be no hope at all.

Dale Carnegie

Wait on the Lord; be of good courage, and he shall strengthen thine heart: wait, I say, on the Lord.

Psalm 27:14

The Lord is my light and my salvation: whom shall I fear? the Lord is the strength of my life; of whom shall I be afraid?

Psalm 27:1

Most of the important things in the world have been accomplished by people who have kept on trying when there seemed to be no hope at all.

Dale Carnegie

Wait on the Lord; be of good courage, and he shall strengthen thine heart: wait, I say, on the Lord.

Psalm 27:14

The Lord is my light and my salvation: whom shall I fear? the Lord is the strength of my life; of whom shall I be afraid?

Psalm 27:1

The Lord is my strength and my shield: my heart trusted in him, and I am helped; therefore my heart greatly rejoiceth; and with my song will I praise him.

Psalm 28:7

Selah!

Let the beloved of the Lord rest secure in him, for he shields him all day long, and the one the Lord loves rests between his shoulders.

Deuteronomy 33:12 NIV

The Lord is my strength and my shield: my heart trusted in him, and I am helped; therefore my heart greatly rejoiceth; and with my song will I praise him.

Psalm 28:7

Selah!

Let the beloved of the Lord rest secure in him, for he shields him all day long, and the one the Lord loves rests between his shoulders.

Deuteronomy 33:12 NIV

People have fallen into the foolish habit of speaking of orthodoxy as something heavy, humdrum and safe. There never was anything so perilous or so exciting as orthodoxy, . . . *It is always easy to let the age have its head; the difficult thing is to keep one's own . . .*

Orthodoxy: The Romance of Faith,
Chesterton

People have fallen into the
foolish habit of speaking of
orthodoxy as something heavy,
humdrum and safe. There
never was anything so perilous
or so exciting as orthodoxy, . . .
It is always easy to let the age
have its head; the difficult
thing is to keep one's own . . .

Orthodoxy: The Romance of Faith,
Chesterton

The only bad thing about makin' a mistake is to keep on makin' it.

James Rupert Nance, Esq.,
1909–1985

There is one thing stronger than all the armies in the world, and that is an idea whose time has come.

Victor Hugo

Nothing in this world is impossible to a willing heart.

Abraham Lincoln

Amen and amen!

The only bad thing about makin' a mistake is to keep on makin' it.

James Rupert Nance, Esq., 1908–1985

There is one thing stronger than all the armies in the world, and that is an idea whose time has come.

Victor Hugo

Nothing in this world is impossible to a willing heart.

Abraham Lincoln

Amen and amen!

Every failure I've ever had is because I said yes when I should have said no.

Loosely adapted from
a remark by Moss Hart

One of the most time-consuming things is to have an enemy.

EB White

If you judge people, you have no time to love them.

Mother Teresa

Every failure I've ever had is
because I said yes when I
should have said no.

Loosely adapted from
a remark by Moss Hart

One of the most time-consuming
things is to have an enemy.

E B White

If you judge people, you have
no time to love them.

Mother Teresa

To write a good love-letter, you ought to begin without knowing what you mean to say, and to finish without knowing what you have written.

Jean-Jacques Rousseau

copy for C

To write a good love—letter,
you ought to begin without
knowing what you mean
to say, and to finish
without knowing what
you have written.

Jean—Jacques Rousseau

copy for C

However confused the scene of our life
appears, however torn we may be who
now do face that scene, it can be faced,
and we can go on to be whole.

Muriel Rukeyser

Talent is always conscious of its own
abundance and does not object to sharing.

Alexander Solzhenitsyn

Thank choir,
thank Avis—

However confused the scene of
our life appears, however torn
we may be who now do face
that scene, it can be faced, and
we can go on to be whole.

Muriel Rukeyser

Talent is always conscious of
its own abundance and does
not object to sharing.

Alexander Solzhenitsyn

Thank
choir,
thank
Avis—

We say we want a renewal of character in our day but we don't really know what we ask for. To have a renewal of character is to have a renewal of a creedal order that constrains, limits, binds, obligates and compels. This price is too high for us to pay. We want character but without conviction; we want strong morality but without the emotional burden of guilt or shame; we want virtue but without particular moral justifications that invariably offend; we want good without having to name evil; we want decency without the authority to

We say we want a renewal of character in our day but we don't really know what we ask for. To have a renewal of character is to have a renewal of a creedal order that constrains, limits, binds, obligates and compels. This price is too high for us to pay. We want character but without conviction; we want strong morality but without the emotional burden of guilt or shame; we want virtue but without particular moral justifications that invariably offend; we want good without having to name evil; we want decency without the authority to insist upon it; we want moral community without any limitations to personal freedom. In short, we want what we cannot possibly have on the terms that we want it.

James Davison Hunter, *The Death of Character: Moral Education in an Age Without Good or Evil*

A real book is not one that we read but one that reads us.

—WH Auden

The most disappointed people in the world are those who get what's coming to them.

Life's Little Instruction Bk

insist upon it; we want moral
community without any
limitations to personal freedom.
In short, we want what we
cannot possibly have on the
terms that we want it.

James Davison Hunter, The Death
of Character: Moral Education
in an Age Without Good or Evil

A real book is not one that we
read but one that reads us.

—WH Auden

The most disappointed people in
the world are those who get
what's coming to them.

Life's Little Instruction Bk

What is the hardest task in the world? To think.

Emerson
Yes!

The poor get poorer by acting rich and the rich get richer by acting poor.

Plaque seen on the wall
of a parishioner

Trouble is a part of your life, and if you don't share it, you don't give the person who loves you a chance to love you enough.

Dinah Shore

(or a chance to love you more?)

What is the hardest task in the world? To think.

Emerson

Yes!

The poor get poorer by acting rich and the rich get richer by acting poor.

Plaque seen on the wall of a parishioner

Trouble is a part of your life, and if you don't share it, you don't give the person who loves you a chance to love you enough.

Dinah Shore

(or a chance to love you more?)

Men often bear little grievances with less courage than they do large misfortunes.

Aesop

It is the sweet, simple things of life which are the real ones after all.

Laura Ingalls Wilder

The best things in life are free.

Cole Porter

Men often bear little grievances
with less courage than they do
large misfortunes.

Aesop

It is the sweet, simple things
of life which are the real ones
after all.

Laura Ingalls Wilder

The best things in life are free.

Cole Porter

Who overcomes by force has overcome
but half his foe.

John Milton

Our tendency is to run from the painful
realities or try to change them as soon as
possible. But *cure without care* makes us
into rulers, controllers, manipulators.

Henri J.M. Nouwen

Who overcomes by force has
overcome but half his foe.

John Milton

Our tendency is to run from
the painful realities or try to
change them as soon as possible.
But _cure without care_ makes
us into rulers, controllers,
manipulators.

Henri J. M. Nouwen

Oswald, Utmost, reading for Dec 18

It is only the loyal soul who believes that God engineers circumstances. . . . we treat the things that happen as if they were engineered by men. To be faithful in every circumstance means that we have only one loyalty, and that is to our Lord.

. . . If we learn to worship God in the trying circumstances, He will alter them in two seconds when He chooses . . .

We will be loyal to work, to service, to anything, but do not

Oswald, Utmost,
   reading for Dec 18

It is only the loyal soul who
believes that God engineers
circumstances. . . . we treat the
things that happen as if they
were engineered by men. To be
faithful in every circumstance
means that we have only one
loyalty, and that is to our Lord.

. . . If we learn to worship God
in the trying circumstances, He
will alter them in two seconds
when He chooses . . .

We will be loyal to work, to
service, to anything, but do not

ask us to be loyal to Jesus Christ . . .

The idea is not that we do work for God, but that we are so loyal to Him that He can do His work through us.

Faith is not belief without proof, but trust without reservation.

Elton Trueblood

Yes!

ask us to be loyal to Jesus
Christ . . .

The idea is not that we do work
for God, but that we are so
loyal to Him that He can do His
work through us.

Faith is not belief without
proof, but trust without
reservation.

                    Elton Trueblood

                         Yes!

At Blackwater Pond the tossed waters
   have settled
after a night of rain.
I dip my cupped hands. I drink
a long time. It tastes
like stone, leaves, fire. It falls cold
into my body, waking the bones. I hear
   them
deep inside me, whispering
oh, what is that beautiful thing
that just happened?

—Mary Oliver, from
"New and Selected Poems"

Copy for C

At Blackwater Pond the tossed waters have settled
after a night of rain.
I dip my cupped hands. I drink
a long time. It tastes
like stone, leaves, fire. It falls cold
into my body, waking the bones. I hear them
deep inside me, whispering
oh, what is that beautiful thing
that just happened?

        --Mary Oliver, from
        "Now and Selected Poems"

copy for C

For as high as the heavens are above the earth, so great is his love for those who fear him; as far as the east is from the west, so far has he removed our transgressions from us.

Ps 103:11–12, NIV

The angel fetched Peter out of prison, but it was prayer that fetched the angel.

Thos Watson *Fetching the Angel*,
June 30, All Saints

I think that gardening is nearer to godliness than theology.

Vigen Guoiran (Sp?),
theologian and gardener

For as high as the heavens are
above the earth, so great is his
love for those who fear him; as
far as the east is from the west,
so far has he removed our
transgressions from us.

Ps 103:11-12, NIV

The angel fetched Peter out of
prison, but it was prayer that
fetched the angel.

Thos Watson Fetching the Angel,
June 30, All Saints

I think that gardening is nearer
to godliness than theology.

Vigen Guroian (Sp?),
theologian and gardener

Once the mind has been stretched by a new idea, it will never again return to its original size.

Oliver W Holmes

Hungry livestock, though in sight of pasture, need the prod.

Heraclitus *trans by Brooks Haxton*

Where there is great love there are always miracles.

Willa Cather

The truly educated never graduate.

Seen on a t-shirt

Once the mind has been
stretched by a new idea, it
will never again return to its
original size.

Oliver W Holmes

Hungry livestock, though in
sight of pasture, need the prod.

Heraclitus trans by Brooks Haxton

Where there is great love there
are always miracles.

Willa Cather

The truly educated
never graduate.

Seen on a t-shirt

The happy childhood is hardly worth your while.

> Frank McCourt in a tv interview

Friendship is forgetting what you give and remembering what you receive.

> *Don't recall source*

The poet John Oxenham said,

Art thou lonely, O my brother?
Share thy little with another!
Stretch a hand to one unfriended,
And thy loneliness is ended.

> Amen and amen,
> *refute that if you can!*

The happy childhood is hardly worth your while.

Frank McCourt in a tv interview

Friendship is forgetting what you give and remembering what you receive.

Don't recall source

The poet John Oxenham said,

Art thou lonely, O my brother?
Share thy little with another!
Stretch a hand to one
unfriended, And thy loneliness
is ended.

Amen and amen,
refute that if you can!

The lowest ebb is the turn of the tide.

Longfellow

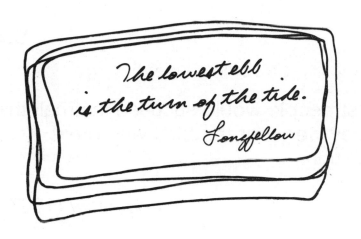

The lowest ebb
is the turn of the tide.

Longfellow

He is a wise man who does not grieve for the things which he has not, but rejoices for those which he has.

Epictetus (c. 50–120)

Selah!

Most people would succeed in small things if they were not troubled with great ambition.

Longfellow (1807–82)

Get into the habit of dealing with God about everything.

Oswald Chambers,
My Utmost for His Highest,
reading for August 23rd

He is a wise man who does not grieve for the things which he has not, but rejoices for those which he has.

Epictetus (c. 50—120)

Selah!

Most people would succeed in small things if they were not troubled with great ambition.

Longfellow (1807—82)

Get into the habit of dealing with God about everything.

Oswald Chambers,
My Utmost for His Highest,
reading for August 23rd

O Lord, in the simplicity of my heart, I offer myself to Thee today, to be Thy servant for ever, to obey Thee, and to be a sacrifice of perpetual praise.

Thomas à Kempis

God is able to make all grace abound to you, so that in all things at all times, having all that you need, you will abound in every good work.

II Corinthians 9:8 NIV

What is the true test of character, unless it be its progressive development in the bustle and turmoil, in the action and reaction of daily life.

Goethe, 1749–1832

O Lord, in the simplicity of
my heart, I offer myself to Thee
today, to be Thy servant for
ever, to obey Thee, and to be a
sacrifice of perpetual praise.

Thomas à Kempis

God is able to make all grace
abound to you, so that in all
things at all times, having all
that you need, you will abound
in every good work.

II Corinthians 9:8 NIV

What is the true test of character,
unless it be its progressive
development in the bustle and
turmoil, in the action and reaction
of daily life.

Goethe, 1749–1832

The contents of someone's bookcase are part of his history, like an ancestral portrait.

Anatole Broyard

The good book is always a book of travel; it is about a life's journey.

HM Tomlinson

I know not how to abstain from reading.

Samuel Pepys

The contents of someone's
bookcase are part of his history,
like an ancestral portrait.

Anatole Broyard

The good book is always a
book of travel; it is about
a life & journey.

H M Tomlinson

I know not how to abstain
from reading.

Samuel Pepys

I've been in love three hundred times in my life, and all but five were with books.

Lee Glickstein

All books are divisible into two classes— the books of the hour, and the books of all time. Mark this distinction: it is not one of quality only . . . it is a distinction of species. There are good books for the hour, and good ones for all time.

John Ruskin, Of Kings' Treasuries

I've been in love three hundred times in my life, and all but five were with books.

Lee Glickstein

All books are divisible into two classes — the books of the hour, and the books of all time. Mark this distinction: it is not one of quality only . . . . it is a distinction of species. There are good books for the hour, and good ones for all time.

John Ruskin, Of Kings' Treasuries

Those who read great works . . . will read the same work ten, twenty or thirty times during the course of their life.

C. S. Lewis,
An Experiment in Criticism

There is no worse robber than a bad book.

Italian proverb

François Mauriac: If you would tell me the heart of a man, tell me not what he reads but what he re-reads.

Those who read great
works . . . will read the same
work ten, twenty or thirty times
during the course of their life.

C. S. Lewis,
An Experiment in Criticism

There is no worse robber than
a bad book.

Italian proverb

François Mauriac:

If you would tell me the heart
of a man, tell me not what he
reads but what he re-reads.

One of the illusions of life is that the present hour is not the critical decisive hour. *Write it on your heart that every day is the best day of the year.*

Ralph Waldo Emerson

Heed this

And this, as well:

First keep the peace within yourself, then you can also bring peace to others.

Thomas à Kempis

Ah! There is nothing like staying at home, for real comfort.

Jane Austen

One of the illusions of life is that the present hour is not the critical decisive hour. Write it on your heart that every day is the best day of the year.

Ralph Waldo Emerson

Heed this

And this, as well:

First keep the peace within yourself, then you can also bring peace to others.

Thomas à Kempis

Ah! There is nothing like staying at home, for real comfort.

Jane Austen

1 Timothy 4:7–8: Train yourselves in godliness, for, while physical training is of some value, godliness is valuable in every way, holding promise for both the present life and the life to come.

Reading the letters of Timothy today, June 28

Be very careful never to forget what you have seen the Lord do for you. Do not let these things escape from your mind as long as you live! And be sure to pass them on to your children and grandchildren.

Deuteronomy 4:9

1 Timothy 4:7-8: Train yourselves in godliness, for, while physical training is of some value, godliness is valuable in every way, holding promise for both the present life and the life to come.

Reading the letters of Timothy today, June 28

Be very careful never to forget what you have seen the Lord do for you. Do not let these things escape from your mind as long as you live! And be sure to pass them on to your children and grandchildren.

Deuteronomy 4:9

People are often unreasonable, illogical, and self-centered.

Forgive them anyway.

If you are kind, people may accuse you of selfish, ulterior motives.

Be kind anyway.

If you are successful, you will win some false friends and some true enemies.

Succeed anyway.

If you are honest and frank, people may cheat you.

Be honest and frank anyway.

What you spend years building, someone could destroy overnight.

Build anyway.

People are often unreasonable,
illogical, and self-centered.

   Forgive them anyway.

If you are kind, people may
accuse you of selfish, ulter-
iior motives.

   Be kind anyway.

If you are successful, you will
win some false friiends and some
true enemies.

   Succeed anyway.

If you are honest and frank, people may cheat you.

   Be honest and frank anyway.

What you spend years building,
someone could destroy overnight.

   Build anyway.

If you find serenity and happiness, there may be jealousy.

   Be happy anyway.

The good you do today, people will often forget tomorrow.

   Be good anyway.

Give the world the best you have, and it may never be enough.

   Give the world the best you have anyway.

You see, in the final analysis, it is between you and (God).

It was never between you and them anyway.

Kent M. Keith

If you find serenity and happiness,
there may be jealousy.
   Be happy anyway.
The good you do today, people will
often forget tomorrow.
   B e good anyway.
Give the world the best you have,
and it may never be enough.
   Give the world the best you have
   anyway.
You see, in the final analysis, it
is between you and (God).
It was never between you and them
anyway.

                    Kent M. Keith

Only he who gives thanks for little things receives the big things. We prevent God from giving us the great spiritual gifts He has in store for us, because we do not give thanks for daily gifts. We think we dare not be satisfied with the small measure of spiritual knowledge, experience, and love that has been given to us, and that we must constantly be looking forward eagerly for the highest good. Then we deplore the fact that we lack the deep certainty, the strong faith, and the rich experience that God has given to others, and we consider this lament to be pious.

Only he who gives thanks for little things receives the big things. We prevent God from giving us the great spiritual gifts He has in store for us, because we do not give thanks for daily gifts. We think we dare not be satisfied with the small measure of spiritual knowledge, experience, and love that has been given to us, and that we must constantly be looking forward eagerly for the highest good. Then we deplore the fact that we lack the deep certainty, the strong faith, and the rich experience that God has given to others, and we consider this lament to be pious.

We pray for the big things, and forget to give thanks daily for the Christian fellowship in which we have been placed, even where there is no great experience, no discoverable riches, but much weakness, small faith, and difficulty; if, on the contrary, we only keep complaining to God that everything is so paltry and petty, so far from what we expected, then we hinder God from letting our fellowship grow according to the measure and riches which are there for us all in Jesus Christ.

Deitrich Bonhoeffer, "Life Together," Harper and Row

We pray for the big things,
and forget to give thanks daily
for the Christian fellowship in
which we have been placed,
even where there is no great
experience, no discoverable riches,
but much weakness, small faith,
and difficulty; if, on the contrary,
we only keep complaining to God
that everything is so paltry and
petty, so far from what we
expected, then we hinder God from
letting our fellowship grow
according to the measure and
riches which are there for us all
in Jesus Christ.

Dietrich Bonhoeffer, "Life Together,"
Harper and Row

Christian brotherhood is not an ideal which we must realize, it is rather a reality created by God in Christ *in which we may participate*.

Ibid.

Discovery consists of seeing what everybody has seen and thinking what nobody has thought.

Albert von Szent-Györgyi

Truth is always exciting. Speak it, then. Life is dull without it.

Pearl Buck

Christian brotherhood is not
an ideal which we must realize,
it is rather a reality created by
God in Christ _in which we_
may participate.

Ibid.

Discovery consists of seeing
what everybody has seen and
thinking what nobody has
thought.

Albert von Szent-Györgyi

Truth is always exciting. Speak
it, then. Life is dull without it.

Pearl Buck

Giving

To give away money is an easy matter, and in any man's power. But to decide to whom to give it, and how large and when, and for what purpose, is neither in every man's power nor an easy matter. Hence it is, that such an excellence is rare, praiseworthy and noble.

Aristotle

The rare individual who unselfishly tries to serve others has an enormous advantage—he has little competition.

Andrew Carnegie

Giving

To give away money is an easy matter, and in any man's power. But to decide to whom to give it, and how large and when, and for what purpose, is neither in every man's power nor an easy matter. Hence it is, that such an excellence is rare, praiseworthy and noble.

Aristotle

The rare individual who unselfishly tries to serve others has an enormous advantage— he has little competition.

Andrew Carnegie

Geo Macdonald, the great inspiration to Lewis, who said, "I have never concealed the fact that I regarded (Macdonald) as my master; indeed I fancy I have never written a book in which I did not quote from him."

B. 1824, Scotland, father 11 children, lectured/preached widely in U.S.

From 3,000 Quotations from the writings of G Macdonald

. . . Never soul was set free without being made to feel its slavery.

Geo Macdonald, the great
inspiration to Lewis, who said,
"I have never concealed the fact
that I regarded (Macdonald)
as my master; indeed I fancy
I have never written a book in
which I did not quote from him."

B. 1824, Scotland, father 11 children,
lectured/preached widely in U.S.

from 3,000 Quotations from
the writings of G Macdonald

... Never soul was set free without
being made to feel its slavery.

. . . The whole trouble is that we won't let God help us.

Yes!

. . . When God can do what He will with a man, the man may do what he will with the world.

. . . There are tender-hearted people who . . . object to the whole scheme of creation; they would neither have force used nor pain suffered; they talk as if kindness could do everything, even where it is not felt. Millions of human beings but for suffering would never develop an atom of affection. The man who would

. . . The whole trouble is that we won't let God help us.

Yes!

. . . When God can do what He will with a man, the man may do what he will with the world.

. . . There are tender-hearted people who . . . object to the whole scheme of creation; they would neither have force used nor pain suffered; they talk as if kindness could do everything, even where it is not felt. Millions of human beings but for suffering would never develop an atom of affection. The man who would spare due suffering is not wise. It is folly to conclude a thing ought not to be done because it hurts. There are powers to be born, creations to be perfected, sinners to be redeemed, through the ministry of pain, that could be born, perfected, redeemed in no other way.

. . . God ministers to us so gently, so stolenly, as it were, with such a quiet, tender, loving absence of display, that men often drink of His wine, as those wedding guests drank, without knowing whence it comes—without thinking that the giver is beside them, yea, in their very hearts.

spare due suffering is not wise.
It is folly to conclude a thing
ought not to be done because it
hurts. There are powers to be
born, creations to be perfected,
sinners to be redeemed, through
the ministry of pain, that could
be born, perfected, redeemed in no
other way.

. . . God ministers to us so
gently, so stolenly, as it were,
with such a quiet, tender, loving
absence of display, that men
often drink of His wine, as those
wedding guests drank, without
knowing whence it comes —
without thinking that the giver
is beside them, yea, in their very
hearts.

. . . Let Him judge us. Posterity may be wiser than we; but posterity is not our judge.

Write the following upon my very forehead!

. . . You have a disagreeable duty to do at twelve o'clock. Do not blacken nine and ten and eleven, and all between, with the color of twelve. Do the work of each, and reap your reward in peace. So when the dreaded moment in the future becomes the present, you shall meet it walking in the light, and that light will overcome its darkness.

. . . Let Him judge us. Posterity may be wiser than we; but posterity is not our judge.

Write the following upon my very forehead!

. . . You have a disagreeable duty to do at twelve o'clock. Do not blacken nine and ten and eleven, and all between, with the color of twelve. Do the work of each, and reap your reward in peace. So when the dreaded moment in the future becomes the present, you shall meet it walking in the light, and that light will overcome its darkness.

No person has ever been honored for what he received. Honor is our reward when we give.

Calvin Coolidge

For by grace you have been saved through faith, and this is not your own doing: it is a gift of God.

Ephesians 2:8

Tithing is a discipleship issue, not a fund-raising issue.

Richard E. Rusbuldt

No person has ever been
honored for what he received.
Honor is our reward when
we give.

Calvin Coolidge

For by grace you have been
saved through faith, and this
is not your own doing: it is a
gift of God.

Ephesians 2:8

Tithing is a discipleship issue,
not a fund-raising issue.

Richard G. Rusbuldt

Like the food supply for an army, prayer simultaneously feeds the individual Christian's spiritual growth and the church's effectiveness in mission. If prayer is not emphasized, both starve.

Herb Miller

I never look at the masses as my responsibility. I look at the individual. I can only love one person at a time.

Mother Teresa

Like the food supply for an army, prayer simultaneously feeds the individual Christian's spiritual growth and the church's effectiveness in mission. If prayer is not emphasized, both starve.

Herb Miller

I never look at the masses as my responsibility. I look at the individual. I can only love one person at a time.

Mother Teresa

Heed this:

(The Word) takes hold of one today and falls into his heart, tomorrow it touches another, and so on. Thus quietly and soberly it will do its work, and no one will know how it all came about.

Martin Luther

Every word of God is pure; he is a shield unto them that put their trust in him.

Prov 30:5

Heed this :

(The Word) takes hold of one
today and falls into his heart,
tomorrow it touches another,
and so on. Thus quietly and
soberly it will do its work, and
no one will know how it all
came about.

                    Martin Luther

Every word of God is pure;
he is a shield unto them
that put their trust in him.

                    Prov 30:5

"I wish you would make up your mind, Mr. Dickens. Was it the best of times or was it the worst of times? It could scarcely have been both."

New Yorker cartoon caption

Sermon fodder re: attitude

"I wish you would make up your mind, Mr. Dickens. Was it the best of times or was it the worst of times? It could scarcely have been both."

New Yorker cartoon caption

Sermon fodder re: attitude

You are a child of your heavenly Father.
Your faith in his love and power can never
be bold enough.

—Basilea Schlink

Be calm in arguing; for fierceness makes
error a fault, and truth discourtesy;
calmness is a great advantage.

—George Herbert

A ship in harbor is safe—but that is not
what ships are made for.

John A. Shedd

You are a child of your
heavenly Father. Your faith
in his love and power can never
be bold enough.

— Basilea Schlink

Be calm in arguing; for fierceness
makes error a fault, and truth
discourtesy; calmness is a great
advantage.

— George Herbert

A ship in harbor is safe — but
that is not what ships are
made for.

John A. Shedd

If I had eight hours to chop down a tree,
I'd spend six sharpening my axe.

Abraham Lincoln

Best sermon
on writing a sermon

If I had eight hours to chop
down a tree, I'd spend six
sharpening my axe.

Abraham Lincoln

Best sermon
on writing a sermon

He was the Word that spake it,
He took the bread and brake it;
And what the Word did make it,
I do believe and take it.

> John Donne, Divine Poems,
> "On the Sacrament"

If you think it's hard to meet new people,
try picking up the wrong golf ball.

> Jack Lemmon

Famous remarks are very seldom quoted
correctly.

> Simeon Strunsky

He was the Word that spake it,
He took the bread and brake it,
And what the Word did make it,
I do believe and take it.

> John Donne, Divine Poems,
> "On the Sacrament"

If you think it's hard to meet
new people, try picking up the
wrong golf ball.

> Jack Lemmon

Famous remarks are very
seldom quoted correctly.

> Simeon Strunsky

Eternal God, I thank you that I am growing old. *It is a privilege that many have been denied* . . . Spare us the self pity that shrivels the soul . . . And grant us daily some moments living on tiptoe, lured by the eternal city . . .

(Author unknown)

Give sorrow words; the grief that does not speak whispers o'er the fraught heart and bids it break.

Macbeth

Yes, yes and ever yes

Eternal God, I thank you that I am growing old. It is a privilege that many have been denied . . . Spare us the self pity that shrivels the soul . . . And grant us daily some moments living on tiptoe, lured by the eternal city . . .

(Author unknown)

Give sorrow words; the grief that does not speak whispers o'er the fraught heart and bids it break.

Macbeth

Yes, yes and ever yes

These prayers from BCP always useful

Prayer of Self-dedication
Almighty and eternal God, so draw our
hearts to thee, so guide our minds, so fill
our imaginations, so control our wills, that
we may be wholly thine, utterly dedicated
unto thee; and then use us, we pray thee,
as thou wilt, and always to thy glory and
the welfare of thy people, through our Lord
and Savior Jesus Christ. Amen.

In the Evening
O Lord, support us all the day long, until
the shadows lengthen, and the evening
comes, and the busy world is hushed and
the fever

These prayers from BCP always useful

Prayer of Self-dedication
Almighty and eternal God, so draw
our hearts to thee, so guide our
minds, so fill our imaginations,
so control our wills, that we may
be wholly thine, utterly dedicated
unto thee; and then use us, we pray
thee, as thou wilt, and always to
thy glory and the welfare of thy
people, through our Lord and
Savior Jesus Christ. Amen

In the Evening
O Lord, support us all the day
long, until the shadows lengthen,
and the evening comes, and the
busy world is hushed and the fever

of life is over, and our work is done. Then in thy mercy, grant us safe lodging, and a holy rest, and peace at the last. Amen.

For a Birthday
O God, our times are in your hand: Look with favor, we pray, on your Servant—as he/she begins another year. Grant that _____ may grow in wisdom and grace, and strengthen his/her trust in your goodness all the days of his/her life; through Jesus Christ our Lord. Amen.

Beautiful, this

of life is over, and our work is
done. Then in thy mercy, grant us
safe lodging, and a holy rest, and
peace at the last. Amen

For a Birthday
O God, our times are in your hand:
Look with favor, we pray, on your
Servant--as he/she begins another
year. Grant that _____ may grow
in wisdom and grace, and strenght-
en his/her trust in your goodness
all the days of his/her life;
through Jesus Christ our Lord.
Amen.

Beautiful, this

For Those We Love

Almighty God, we entrust all who are dear to us to thy never-failing care and love, for this life and the life to come, knowing that thou art doing for them better things than we can desire or pray for; through Jesus Christ our Lord. Amen

For Those We Love

Almighty God, we entrust all who
are dear to us to thy never-
failing care and love, for
thiis life and the life to come,
knowing that thou art doing for
them better thiings than we can
desire or pray for; through Jesus
Christ our Lord. Amen

For Towns and Rural Areas

Lord Christ, when you came among us you proclaimed the kingdom of God in villages, towns, and lonely places: Grant that your presence and power may be known throughout this land. Have mercy upon all of us who live and work in rural areas, especially Mitford, Farmer, Wesley, and the Valley, and grant that all the people of our nation may give thanks to you for food and drink and all other bodily necessities of life, respect those who labor to produce them, and honor the land and the water from which these good things come. All this we ask in your holy Name. Amen.

For Towns and Rural Areas

Lord Christ, when you came among us you proclaimed the kingdom of God in villages, towns, and lonely places: Grant that your peesence and power may be known throughout this land. Have mercy upon all of us who live and work in rural areas, exspecially Mitford, Farmer, Wesley, and the Valley, and grant that all the people of our nation may give thanks to you for food and driink and all other bodily necessities of life, respect those who labor to produce them, and honor the land and the water from which these good things come. All thiis we ask in your holy Name. Amen

For our Country

Almighty God, who hast given us this good land for our heritage: We humbly beseech thee that we may always prove ourselves a people mindful of thy favor and glad to do thy will. Bless our land with honorable industry, sound learning, and pure manners. Save us from violence, discord, and confusion; from pride and arrogance, and from every evil way. Defend our liberties, and fashion into one united people the multitudes brought hither out of many kindreds and tongues. Endue with the spirit of wisdom those to whom in thy Name we entrust the authority of government, that there

For our Country

Almighty God, who hast given us
this good land for our heritage:
We humbly beseech thee that we
may always prove ourselves a
people mindful of thy favor and
glad to do thy will. Bless our
land with honorable iindustry,
sound learning, and pure manners.
Save us from violence, discord,
and confusion; from pride and
arrogance, and from every evil way.
Defend our liberties, and fashion
into one united people the multitudes brought hither out of many
kindreds and tongues. Endue with
the spirit of wiisdom those to
whom in thy Name we entrust the
authority of government, that there

may be justice and peace at home, and that, through obedience to thy law, we may show forth thy praise, among the nations of the earth. In the time of prosperity, fill our hearts with thankfulness, and in the day of trouble suffer not our trust in thee to fail; all which we ask through Jesus Christ our Lord. Amen.

may be justice and peace at home,
and that, through obedience to thy
law, we may show forth thy praise,
among the nations of the earth.
In the time of prosperity, fill
our hearts with thankfulness, and
iin the day of trouble suffer not
our trust in thee to fail; all
which we ask through Jesus Christ
our Lord.   Amen

From Gary Barnes' little paper over the mtn.

How to keep a healthy level of sanity:
As often as possible, skip rather than walk.
Sing along at the opera.
When the money comes out of the ATM, yell "I won! I won!"
Page yourself over the intercom—don't disguise your voice.
Every time someone asks you to do something, ask if they want fries with it.
Specify that your drive-through order is "to go."

Send to Stuart,
Fr Roland

From Gary Barnes' little paper
over the mtn.

How to keep a healthy level of
sanity:
As often as possible, skip rather
than walk.
Sing along at the opera.
When the money comes out of
the ATM, yell "I won! I won!"
Page yourself over the intercom—
don't disguise your voice.
Every time someone asks you to
do something, ask if they want
fries with it.
Specify that your drive-through
order is "to go."

Send to Stuart,
Fr Roland

I pray that the God of our Lord Jesus Christ, the all-glorious Father, may confer on you the spiritual gifts of wisdom and vision, with the knowledge of him that they bring. I pray that your inward eyes may be enlightened, so that you may know what is the hope to which he calls you, how rich and glorious is the share he offers you among his people in their inheritance, and how vast are the resources of his power open to us who have faith.

Ephesians 1:17–19, REB
The Resources of Power, Nov. 18,
St. Luke's

I pray that the God of our Lord Jesus Christ, the all-glorious Father, may confer on you the spiritual gifts of wisdom and vision, with the knowledge of him that they bring. I pray that your inward eyes may be enlightened, so that you may know what is the hope to which he calls you, how rich and glorious is the share he offers you among his people in their inheritance, and how vast are the resources of his power open to us who have faith.

Ephesians 1:17–19, RGB
The Resources of Power, Nov. 18, St. Luke's

Never consider whether you are of use, but ever consider that you are not your own but His.

Oswald Chambers

Choose a job you love and you will never work a day in your life.

Confucius

A cat could very well be man's best friend but would never stoop to admitting it.

Doug Larson

The way I see it, if you want the rainbow, you got to put up with the rain.

Dolly Parton

Never consider whether you are
of use, but ever consider that
you are not your own but His.

Oswald Chambers

Choose a job you love and
you will never work a day
in your life.

Confucius

A cat could very well be man's
best friend but would never
stoop to admitting it.

Doug Larson

The way I see it, if you want the
rainbow, you got to put up
with the rain.

Dolly Parton

As in the clay emerging from the fire a
  vessel
Laughter is the shortest distance between
  two people.

Victor Borge

There's nothing a man can do to improve
himself so much as writing his memoirs.

Anon

It is impossible to mentally or socially
enslave a Bible-reading people.

Horace Greeley

As in the clay emerging from
        the fire a vessel
Laughter is the shortest
        distance between two people.
                              Victor Borge

There's nothing a man can do
to improve himself so much as
writing his memoirs.
                              Anon

It is impossible to mentally or
socially enslave a Bible—reading
people.
                              Horace Greeley

Did you ever notice that when you blow
into a dog's face he gets mad, but when
you take him in a car he sticks his head
out the window?

Steve Bluestein

The best way out is always through.

Robert Frost

Amen and amen

Use what talents you possess—
the woods would be very silent
if no birds sang there
except those that sang best.

Henry Van Dyke

Did you ever notice that when you blow into a dog's face he gets mad, but when you take him in a car he sticks his head out the window?

Steve Bluestein

The best way out is always through.

Robert Frost

Amen and amen

Use what talents you possess—
the woods would be very silent
if no birds sang there
except those that sang best.

Henry Van Dyke

From Oswald Chambers, *My Utmost for His Highest*

"We must distinguish between the burden-bearing that is right and the burden-bearing that is wrong. We ought never to bear the burden of sin or of doubt, but there are burdens placed on us by God which He does not intend to lift off. He wants us to roll them back on Him. If we undertake work for God and get out of touch with Him, the sense of responsibility will be overwhelmingly crushing; but if we roll back on God that which He has put upon us, He takes away the sense of responsibility by bringing in the realization of Himself.

"Many workers have gone out with high courage and fine impulses,

From Oswald Chambers, <u>My Utmost</u>
   <u>for His Highest</u>

"We must distinguish between the
burden-bearing that is riight and
the burden-bearing that is wrong.
We ought never to bear the burden
of siin or of doubt, but there
are burdens placed on us by God
which He does not intend to lift
off. He wants us to roll them back
on Him. If we undertake work for
God and get out of touch with Him,
the sense of responsibiility will
be overwhelmingly crushing; but
if we roll back on God that which
He has put upon us, He takes away
the responsibility by bringing in
the realization of Himself.

"Many workers have gone out wi th
high courage and fine impulses,

but with no intimate fellowship with Jesus Christ, and before long they are crushed. They do not know what to do with the burden, it produces weariness, and people say, What an embittered end to such a beginning!

"Roll thy burden upon the Lord—you have been bearing it all; deliberately put one end on the shoulders of God. 'The government shall be upon His shoulders.' Commit to God 'that He hath given thee'; not fling it off, but put it over on to Him, and yourself with it, and the burden is lightened by the sense of companionship. Never disassociate yourself from the burden."

but with no intiimate fellowship
with Jesus Christ, and before long
they are crushed. They do not know
what to do with the burden, it
produces weariness, and people say,
What an embittered end to such a
beginning!

"Roll thy burden upon the Lord--
you have been bearing it all;
deliberately put one end on the
shoulders of God. 'The government shall be upon His shoulders.'
Commit to God 'that He hath given
Thee'; not fling iit off, but put
it over on to Him, and yourself
with it, and the burden is lightened by the sense of companionnship.
Never disassociate yourself from
the burden.

God reminds us of the past lest we get into a shallow security in the present . . . our yesterdays present irreparable things to us; it is true that we have lost opportunities which will never return, but God can transform this destructive anxiety into a constructive thoughtfulness for the future. *Let the past sleep, but let it sleep on the bosom of Christ . . .*

Ministering as opportunity surrounds us does not mean selecting our surroundings, it means being very selectly God's in any haphazard surroundings which He engineers for us.

God reminds us of the past lest
we get into a shallow security in
the present . . . our yesterdays
present irreparable thiings to us;
it is true that we have lost oppor-
tuniities which will never return,
but God can transform this destructive anxiety into a constructive
thoughtfulness for the future.
Let the past sheep, but let it
sleep on the bosom of Christ . . .

Ministoring as opportunity surrounds
us does not mean selecting our surroundings, it means being very
selectly God's in any haphazard
surroundings which He engineers
for us.

Watch the kind of people God brings around you, and you will be humiliated to find that this is His way of revealing to you the kind of person you have been to Him. *Now, He says, exhibit to that one exactly what I have shown to you.*

> Ibid. Sermon 3/24 The Platinum Rule, i.e., do unto others as God has done unto you

Worship aright in your private relationships, then when God sets you free you will be ready . . .

Abandon to God is of more value than personal holiness. Personal holiness focuses the eye on our own whiteness; we are greatly concerned about the way we walk and talk and look, fearful lest we

Watch the kind of pepple God brings
around you, and you wiill be humiliated to find that thiis is His
way of revealing to you the kind
of person you have been to Him.
Now, He says, exhibit to that one
exactly what I have shown to you.

> Ibid. Sermon 3/24 The Platinum
> Rule, i.e., do unto others as
> God has done unto you

Worship ariight in your private
relationships, then when God sets
you free you will be ready . . .

Abandon to God is of more value
than personal holiness. Personal
holiness focuses the eye on our
own whiteness; we are greatly con0
cerned about the way we walk and
talk and look, fearful lest we

offend Him. Perfect love casts out all that when once we are abandoned to God. We have to get rid of this notion—"Am I of any use?" and make up our minds that we are not, and we may be near the truth. It is never a question of being of use, but of being of value to God Himself. When we are abandoned to God, He works through us all the time.

Beware of not acting upon what you see in your moments on the mount with God. If you do not obey the light, it will turn into darkness.

offend Him. Perfect love casts out
all that when øⱥⱥ once we are abandoned to God. We have to get rid
of this notion--"Am I of any use?"
and make up our minds that we are
not, and we may be near the truth.
It is never a question of being
of use, but of being of value to
God Himself. When we are abandoned
to God, He works through us all
the time.

B eware of not acting upon what
you see in your momentson the
mount with God. If you do not
obey the liight, it will turn
into darkness.

If little labour, little are our gaines;
Man's fortunes are according to his paines.

Robt Herrick

The contemporary proverb, No pain, no
gain, not so contemporary

He is no fool who gives what he cannot
keep to gain what he cannot lose.

Jim Elliot

We are always doing something for
Posterity, but I would fain see Posterity do
something for us.

Joseph Addison Stuart

If little labour, little are our gaines;
Man's fortunes are according to
       his paines.
                         Robt Herrick

The contemporary proverb,
No pain, no gain, not so
contemporary

He is no fool who gives what he
cannot keep to gain what he
cannot lose.

                         Jim Elliot

We are always doing something
for Posterity, but I would fain
see Posterity do something for us.

                    Joseph Addison Stuart

Will Rogers:
The quickest way to double your money is to fold it over and put it back in your pocket.

Never miss a good chance to shut up.

You can observe a lot just by watching.

Yogi Berra

Outside of a dog, a book is a man's best friend. Inside of a dog, it's too dark to read.

Groucho Marx

If it weren't for electricity, we'd all be watching television by candlelight.

George Gobel

Will Rogers:

The quickest way to double your money is to fold it over and put it back in your pocket.

Never miss a good chance to shut up.

You can observe a lot just by watching.

Yogi Berra

Outside of a dog, a book is a man's best friend. Inside of a dog, it's too dark to read.

Groucho Marx

If it weren't for electricity, we'd all be watching television by candlelight.

George Gobel

I have enough money to last me the rest of my life—unless I buy something.

Jackie Mason

Nothing is more responsible for the good old days than a bad memory.

Robert Benchley

Age is a high price to pay for maturity.

Tom Stoppard

I enjoy convalescence. It's the part that makes the illness worthwhile.

G. Bernard Shaw

I have enough money to last
me the rest of my life unless I
buy something.

Jackie Mason

Nothing is more responsible for
the good old days than a bad
memory.

Robert Benchley

Age is a high price to pay for
maturity.

Tom Stoppard

I enjoy convalescence. It's the
part that makes the illness
worthwhile.

G. Bernard Shaw

You know you're getting old when you stoop to tie your shoes and wonder what else you can do while you're down there.

George Burns

I'm not bald, I'm just taller than my hair.

Thom Sharpe

One disadvantage of having nothing to do is you can't stop and rest.

Franklin P. Jones

Grown-up people really ought to be more careful. Among themselves it may seem but a small thing to give their word and take (it back).

Kenneth Grahame

You know you're getting old
when you stoop to tie your shoes
and wonder what else you can
do while you're down there.

George Burns

I'm not bald, I'm just taller
than my hair.

Thom Sharpe

One disadvantage of having
nothing to do is you can't stop
and rest.

Franklin P. Jones

Grown-up people really ought
to be more careful. Among
themselves it may seem but a
small thing to give their word
and take (it back).

Kenneth Grahame

Life is this simple: We are living in a world that is absolutely transparent, and God is shining through it all the time. This is not just a fable or a nice story. It is true. If we abandon ourselves to God and forget ourselves, we see it sometimes, and we see it maybe frequently. God shows Himself everywhere, in everything—in people and in things and in nature and in events . . . we cannot be without Him. It's impossible. The only thing is, we don't see it.

Thos Merton, 20th c Catholic monk

Life is this simple: We are living in a world that is absolutely transparent, and God is shining through it all the time. This is not just a fable or a nice story. It is true. If we abandon ourselves to God and forget ourselves, we see it sometimes, and we see it maybe frequently. God shows Himself everywhere, in everything—in people and in things and in nature and in events . . . we cannot be without Him. It's impossible. The only thing is, we don't see it.

Thos Merton, 20th c Catholic monk

To love at all is to be vulnerable. Love anything, and your heart will certainly be wrung and possibly be broken. If you want to make sure of keeping it intact, you must give your heart to no one. It will not be broken; it will become unbreakable, impenetrable, irredeemable. The alternative to tragedy, or at least to the risk of tragedy, is damnation. The only place outside of heaven where you can be perfectly safe from all the dangers and perturbations of love is Hell.

C. S. Lewis, The Four Loves

To love at all is to be vulnerable. Love anything, and your heart will certainly be wrung and possibly be broken. If you want to make sure of keeping it intact, you must give your heart to no one. It will not be broken; it will become unbreakable, impenetrable, irredeemable. The alternative to tragedy, or at least to the risk of tragedy, is damnation. The only place outside of heaven where you can be perfectly safe from all the dangers and perturbations of love is Hell.

C. S. Lewis, The Four Loves

Love must be as much a light as it is a flame.

Thoreau

But none of these things move me; nor do I count my life dear to myself, so that I may finish my race with joy, and the ministry which I received from the Lord Jesus, to testify to the gospel of the grace of God.

Acts 20:24

"And in every work that he began in the service of the house of God . . . he did it with all his heart, and prospered."

II Chronicles 31:21

Love must be as much a light
as it is a flame.

Thoreau

But none of these things move
me; nor do I count my life dear
to myself, so that I may finish
my race with joy, and the
ministry which I received from
the Lord Jesus, to testify to the
gospel of the grace of God.

Acts 20:34

"And in every work that he
began in the service of the house
of God . . . he did it with all
his heart, and prospered."

II Chronicles 31:21

The process of being made broken bread and poured out wine means that you have to be nourishment for other souls until they learn to feed on God. . . . Be careful that you get your supply, or before long you will be utterly exhausted. . . . Be exhausted for God, but remember your supply comes from Him. "All my fresh springs shall be in Thee."

Utmost, reading for Feb 9

The process of being made broken bread and poured out wine means that you have to be nourishment for other souls until they learn to feed on God. . . . Be careful that you get your supply, or before long you will be utterly exhausted. . . . Be exhausted for God, but remember your supply comes from Him. "All my fresh springs shall be in Thee."

Utmost, reading for Feb 9

Few things help an individual more than to place responsibility on him, and let him know that you trust him.

> Booker T. Washington, 1856–1915

Who knows better than He how to guide our mind and pen for His design?

> John Bunyan

August 19: Nine essays roughly completed

Few things help an individual
more than to place responsibility
on him, and let him know that
you trust him.

Booker T. Washington, 1856—1915

Who knows better than He how
to guide our mind and pen for
His design?

John Bunyan

August 19: Nine essays roughly
completed

Prayer is an effort of will. After we have entered our secret place and have shut the door, the most difficult thing to do is to pray; we cannot get our minds into working order, and the first thing that conflicts is wandering thoughts. . . . We must have a settled place for prayer, and when we get there, the plague of flies begins—This must be done, that must be done.

August 23rd, Utmost

Prayer is an effort of will. After we have entered our secret place and have shut the door, the most difficult thing to do is to pray; we cannot get our minds into working order, and the first thing that conflicts is wandering thoughts. . . . We must have a settled place for prayer, and when we get there, the plague of flies begins— This must be done, that must be done.

August 23rd, Utmost

It took me 15 years to discover that I had no talent for writing, but I couldn't give it up because by that time I was too famous.

—Robert Benchley

12/1 Have discovered early on that I have no talent for writing essays, and have today given up the miserable ordeal entirely, *thanks be to God!*

An insufficient talent is the cruelest of all temptations.

George Moore

It took me 15 years to discover
that I had no talent for
writing, but I couldn't give it
up because by that time I was
too famous.

— Robert Benchley

12/1   Have discovered early on
that I have no talent for writing
essays, and have today given up
the miserable ordeal entirely,
thanks be to God!

An insufficient talent is the
cruelest of all temptations.

George Moore

From Macbeth:

Cans't thou not minister to a mind diseas'd, pluck from the memory a rooted sorrow, raze out the written troubles of the brain, and with some sweet oblivious antidote cleanse the . . . bosom of that perilous stuff which weights upon the heart?

from Macbeth:

Canst thou not minister
to a mind diseas'd, pluck
from the memory a rooted
sorrow, raze out the written
troubles of the brain, and
with some sweet oblivious
antidote cleanse the . . .
bosom of that perilous
stuff which weights upon
the heart?

Evening prayer:

Watch O Lord, with those who wake, or watch, or weep tonight, and give your angels and saints charge over those who sleep. Tend your sick ones, O Lord Christ. Rest Your weary ones, Bless Your dying ones. Soothe Your suffering ones. Pity your afflicted ones, shield Your joyous ones. And all for your love's sake.

St Augustine

Evening prayer:

Watch O Lord, with those
who wake, or watch, or weep
tonight, and give your angels
and saints charge over those
who sleep. Tend your sick ones,
O Lord Christ. Rest Your weary
ones, Bless Your dying ones.
Soothe Your suffering ones. Pity
your afflicted ones, shield Your
joyous ones. And all for your
love's sake.

St Augustine

Keep a clear eye toward life's end. Do not forget your purpose and destiny as God's Creature. What you are in His sight is what you are and nothing more. Remember that when you leave this earth, you can take nothing you have received . . . but only what you have given; a full heart enriched by honest service, love, sacrifice and courage.

Francis of Assisi

Keep a clear eye toward life's end.
Do not forget your purpose and
destiny as God's Creature. What
you are in His sight is what
you are and nothing more.
Remember that when you leave
this earth, you can take nothing
you have received . . . but only
what you have given; a full
heart enriched by honest service,
love, sacrifice and courage.

Francis of Assisi

Ancora imparo
(I am still learning).

—Michelangelo,
at age 87

Ancora imparo
(I am still learning).

— Michelangelo,
at age 87

Lilies:
    Ariadne, Turkscap, fragrant
    White/rose band/maroon spotting
    4–6 ft stems, for bed at garage?
    White Butterflies, profusely flowering,
    vigorous
    Casa Blanca, La Claridad
    Speciosum rubrum, fragrant, late-
    summer, white/crimson
    Trumpet lily: Amethyst Temple, fragrant,
    blooms mid-July

Cty agent re: soil test
Hood's Nursery re: copper sulfate for
peonies?

Hemerocallis:
Chorus Line, Along the Way, both glorious,
new bed at street

Lilies:

Ariadne, Turkscap, fragrant
white / rose band / maroon
spotting
4 – 6 ft stems, for bed at garage?
White Butterflies, profusely
flowering, vigorous
Casa Blanca, La Claridad
Speciosum rubrum, fragrant,
late-summer, white / crimson
Trumpet lily: Amethyst Temple,
fragrant, blooms mid-July

Cty agent re: soil test
Hood's Nursery re: copper sulfate
for peonies?

Hemerocallis:
Chorus Line, Along the Way,
both glorious, new bed at street

Hosta: pp. 86, Emerald Atoll, miniature, for
  naturalizing
Trumpet narcissus, Empress of Ireland,
  white
Double Narcissus: Sir Winston Churchill (6
  bulbs Andrew, 6 Stuart, 6 Helene, 12
  Lord's Chapel garden)
Double Tulips: Angelique, Maywonder (12
  Lord's Chapel)
Adenophora, Artemisia, alcea, astilbe
Peonies: Lady Alexandra Duff, Festiva
  Maxima
Papaver: Royal Wedding, Garden Glory
Phlox? *Ask C*

Hosta: pp. 86, Emerald Atoll,
     miniature, for naturalizing
Trumpet narcissus,
     Empress of Ireland, white
Double Narcissus: Sir Winston
     Churchill (6 bulbs Andrew,
     6 Stuart, 6 Helene, 12 Lord's
     Chapel garden)
Double Tulips: Angelique,
     Maywonder (12 Lord's Chapel)
Adenophora, Artemisia, alcea,
     astilbe
Peonies: Lady Alexandra Duff,
     Festiva Maxima
Papaver: Royal Wedding, Garden
     Glory

Phlox? Ask C

eggs lamb chops salmon red potatoes
salad grns tea bags apples oranges
bananas grpfrt ww bread avocado
yellow onions (3) chckn stock (2)
lemon jello (2) 6-pak V-8

Barnabas: Shots 6/22, 4 p.m.
HEART WORM PILLS

Hoppy, Wednesday 4:30
Remembering Miss Sadie, June 14

Yr server has unexpectedly terminated the
connection?
Server cannot be found?

Ask Marge

eggs lamb chops salmon
red potatoes salad grns tea bags
apples oranges bananas yogrt
ww bread avocado
yellow onions (3) chckn stock (2)
lemon Jell-o (2) 6-pak V-8

Barnabas: Shots 6/22, 4 p.m.
HEART WORM PILLS

Hoppy, Wednesday 4:30
Remembering Miss Sadie, June 14

Yr server has unexpectedly
terminated the connection?
Server cannot be found?
                    Ask Marge

E-mail Emma re: daughter's Atlanta address

Steak (Call Avis)

Pie shells, choc pud, Hershey kisses
Oysters, two pints (Avis, reserve)
Cracker crumbs
Nutmeg
Heavy cream
10-lb ham, bone in (ordered)
fresh coconut

Oranges, tangerines, cherries, et al for
   ambrosia
Sweet potatoes (8 lg.)
Brn sugar
Butter
Eggs
Cider
Cranberries
Romaine
Parmesan
1/2 doz lemons

E-mail Emma re: daughter's Atlanta address

Steak (Call Avis)

Pie shells, choc pud, Hershey kisses

Oysters, two pints (Avis, reserve)

Cracker crumbs

Nutmeg

Heavy cream

10-lb ham, bone in (ordered)

fresh coconut

Oranges, tangerines, cherries, et al. for ambrosia

Sweet potatoes (8 lg.)

Brn sugar

Butter

Eggs

Cider

Cranberries

Romaine

Parmesan

1/2 doz lemons

Dooley, digital camera, done

Shirt, belt, pants, raincoat, done

Sammy, cableknit sweater, L

Sissy/Sassy, back packs
    Ltl Women, Narnia, N. Drew, Wind in
    Willows, Miss Rumphius, Grn Gables
    boxed set

Puny, crock pot

Nurses @ Hope House, chocolates, 4 dzn,
reserved at Local Children's Hosp., as
above, check before end month

Dooley, digital camera, done

Shirt, belt, pants, raincoat, done

Sammy, cableknit sweater, £

Sissy/Sassy, back packs
   Ltl Women, Narnia,
      N. Drew, Wind in Willows,
         Miss Rumphius, Grn Gables
      boxed set

Puny, crock pot

Nurses @ Hope House, chocolates,
   4 dzn, reserved at Local
      Children's Hosp., as above,
      check before end month

Andrew, my cpy early Oxfd Bk Eng Verse

Fred, Garden spade, Dora's Hdwe, on
   order

Jonathan Tolson and siblings, gft certif.

Miss Pattie, warm socks Done

Ben Isaac, Bach CD Done

Poo, Jessie   Game, books done

Walter/Kat   lthr bound guest book,
   ordered

Owens   Travel diary, ordered

Andrew, my cpy early Oxfd Bk
Eng Verse

Fred, Garden spade, Dora's
Hdwe, on order

Jonathan Tolson and siblings,
gft certif.

Miss Pattie, warm socks   Done

Ben Isaac, Bach CD   Done

Poo, Jessie Game, books done
Walter/Kat lthr bound guest
book, ordered

Owens Travel diary, ordered

Louella, housecoat, L with zippered front
Lipstick, done

Lon Burtie, book on orchids, ordered

Fr Roland et al, ham, ordered

Stuart, book on cathedrals, ordered

Scott, dog treats

C, silk pjs., robe, ordered

Louella, housecoat, L with
   zippered front
Lipstick, done

Lon Curtie, book on orchids,
                              ordered

Fr Roland et al, ham, ordered

Stuart, book on cathedrals,
   ordered

Scott, dog treats ✓

C, silk pjs., robe, ordered

Lew Boyd's ice box pickle recipe, makes two qts.

2 cps cider vinegar
2 cps water
1 cp sugar
2 tablesp salt
cucumbers
1 small onion sliced
1 garlic clove chopped

Combine vinegar, water, sugar and salt. Bring to boil. Take off heat and let cool. Wash, peel and slice cukes. Place onion and garlic in jar. Add cukes, filling jar to top. Fill with vinegar mixture and seal. Refrigerate three days, keep unused portion in fridge. Can re-use the vinegar in later batches.

Lew Boyd's ice box pickle recipe,
makes two qts.
  2 cps cider vinegar
  2 cps water
  1 cp sugar
  2 tablesp salt
  cucumbers
  1 small onion sliced
  1 garlic clove chopped

Combine vinegar, water, sugar
and salt. Bring to boil. Take off
heat and let cool. Wash, peel
and slice cukes. Place onion and
garlic in jar. Add cukes, filling
jar to top. Fill with vinegar
mixture and seal. Refrigerate
three days, keep unused portion
in fridge. Can re—use the vinegar
in later batches.

Tape of Absalom's sermon at LC to Lottie Greer

Mazda: change oil, rotate tires, filters, wiper blades

Mustang: Seat belt driver's side, ask Lew— balance front tires

Snow:

12/24
12/29
1/13
1/26
2/10
3/14 Alleluia! Narcissus pushing up through fresh snow

Tape of Absalom's sermon
at LC to Lottie Green

Mazda: change oil, rotate tires,
filters, wiper blades

Mustang: Seat belt driver's side,
ask Lew — balance front tires

Snow:
  12/24
  12/29
  1/13
  1/26
  2/10
  3/14 Alleluia! Narcissus
  pushing up through
fresh snow

Father Timothy Andrew Kavanagh is the principal character in author Jan Karon's series of bestselling Mitford novels, set in a mountain village in western North Carolina. Father Tim is a sixtysomething Episcopal priest beloved by all for his unfailing concern for their needs, and for his exceptional warmth, grace, charm, and devotion to God.

In this second volume of his quote books, Father Tim has recorded favorite wisdom from a variety of thinkers, philosophers, and poets who have enlisted his admiration over the years.

For my legions of Mitford readers, and
all who come to this volume:

*May the Lord, the God of your fathers,
increase you a thousand times and bless
you as he has promised.*

Deuteronomy 1:11 NIV

OTHER MITFORD BOOKS BY JAN KARON

At Home in Mitford
A Light in the Window
These High, Green Hills
Out to Canaan
A New Song
A Common Life
Shepherds Abiding
Patches of Godlight
The Mitford Snowmen
Esther's Gift

CHILDREN'S BOOKS

Miss Fannie's Hat
Jeremy: The Tale of an Honest Bunny

BOOKS FOR ALL AGES

The Trellis and the Seed

Coming in 2005:
Light from Heaven
the ninth novel in Jan Karon's
bestselling Mitford series

This Large Print Edition, prepared especially for Doubleday Large Print Home Library, contains the complete, unabridged text of the original Publisher's Edition.

VIKING

Published by the Penguin Group
Penguin Group (USA) Inc., 375 Hudson Street, New York, New York 10014, U.S.A.
Penguin Group (Canada), 10 Alcorn Avenue, Toronto, Ontario, Canada M4V 3B2
(a division of Pearson Penguin Canada Inc.)
Penguin Books Ltd, 80 Strand, London WC2R 0RL, England
Penguin Ireland, 25 St. Stephen's Green, Dublin 2, Ireland
(a division of Penguin Books Ltd)
Penguin Books Australia Ltd, 250 Camberwell Road, Camberwell, Victoria 3124, Australia
(a division of Pearson Australia Group Pty Ltd)
Penguin Books India Pvt Ltd, 11 Community Centre, Panchsheel Park, New Delhi—110 017, India
Penguin Group (NZ), Cnr Airborne and Rosedale Roads, Albany, Auckland 1310, New Zealand
(a division of Pearson New Zealand Ltd)
Penguin Books (South Africa) (Pty) Ltd, 24 Sturdee Avenue, Rosebank, Johannesburg 2196, South Africa

Penguin Books Ltd, Registered Offices: 80 Strand, London WC2R 0RL, England

First published in 2005 by Viking Penguin, a member of Penguin Group (USA) Inc.

Copyright © Jan Karon, 2005
All rights reserved

ISBN 0-7394-5504-4
Printed in the United States of America

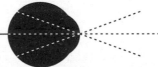

This Large Print Book carries the
Seal of Approval of N.A.V.H.